Molière Les Précieuses Ridicules

Molière

𝕮𝖑𝖆𝖗𝖊𝖓𝖉𝖔𝖓 𝕻𝖗𝖊𝖘𝖘 𝕾𝖊𝖗𝖎𝖊𝖘

MOLIÈRE'S

LES PRÉCIEUSES RIDICULES

LANG

London

HENRY FROWDE

OXFORD UNIVERSITY PRESS WAREHOUSE

AMEN CORNER

LES PRECIEUSES RIDICULES.

Clarendon Press Series

MOLIÈRE'S

LES

PRÉCIEUSES RIDICULES

EDITED

WITH INTRODUCTION AND NOTES

BY

ANDREW LANG, M.A.

Late Fellow of Merton College

Oxford

AT THE CLARENDON PRESS

1884

CONTENTS.

PREFATORY NOTE.

THIS volume is one of a series of French Plays, the editors of which have been good enough to adopt the plan of the edition of *Horace* published by me in the Clarendon Press Series, to permit me to read their proofs, and to admit among their work an 'Essay on the Progress of French Comedy,' which takes the place of those on Tragedy in the *Horace*. For this Essay I alone am responsible, as well as for the non-detection of any oversights in the remaining Prolegomena and the Notes, which are the work of the several editors, and the credit of which is solely due to them.

GEORGE SAINTSBURY.

I HAVE to thank the Editors and Publishers of the *Encyclopaedia Britannica* for leave to reprint a slightly abridged form of my Life of Molière, in the *Encyclopaedia*.

A. LANG.

PROLEGOMENA.

I. LIFE OF MOLIÈRE.

MOLIÈRE, to give Jean Baptiste Poquelin the stage name
which he chose, for some undiscovered reason, to assume,
was born in Paris, probably in January, 1622. The baptismal
certificate which is usually, and almost with absolute cer-
tainty, accepted as his is dated January 15, 1622 ; but it is
not possible to infer that he was born on the day of his
christening. The exact place of his birth is also disputed ;
but it seems tolerably certain that he saw the light in a house
of the Rue St. Honoré. His father was Jean Poquelin, an
upholsterer, who, in 1631, succeeded his own uncle as *valet
tapissier de chambre du Roi.* The family of Poquelin came
from Beauvais, where, for some centuries, they had been
prosperous tradesmen. The legend of their Scotch descent
seems to have been finally disproved by the researches of
M. E. Révérend du Mesnil. The mother of Molière was
Marie Cressé. On his father's side Molière was connected
with the family of Mazuel, musicians attached to the Court of
France. In 1632 Molière lost his mother; his father married
again in 1633. The father possessed certain shops in the
covered Halle de la Foire Saint Germain des Près, and the
biographers conjecture that Molière might have received his
first bent towards the stage from the spectacles offered to the
holiday people at the Fair. Of his early education little is
known ; but it is certain that his mother possessed a Bible
and Plutarch's *Lives*, books which an intelligent child would
not fail to study. In spite of a persistent tradition, there is
no reason to believe that the later education of Molière was
neglected. ' Il fit ses humanitez au Collège de Clermont,'
says the brief life of the comedian published by his friend
and fellow-actor, La Grange, in the edition of his works

printed in 1682. La Grange adds that Molière 'eut l'advantage de suivre M. le Prince de Conti dans toutes ses classes.'
As Conti was seven years younger than Molière, it is not
easy to understand how Molière came to be the school contemporary of the prince. Among more serious studies the
Jesuit fathers encouraged their pupils to take part in *ballets*,
and in later life Molière was a distinguished master of this
sort of entertainment. According to Grimarest, the first
writer who published a life of Molière in any detail (1705),
he not only acquired his 'humanities,' but finished his 'philosophy' in five years. He left the Collège de Clermont in 1641,
the year when Gassendi, a great contemner of Aristotle,
arrived in Paris. The Logic and Ethics of Aristotle, with
his Physics and Metaphysics, were the chief philosophical
text-books at the Collège de Clermont. But when Molière
became the pupil of Gassendi (in company with Cyrano de
Bergerac, Chapelle, and Hesnaut), he was taught to appre-
ciate the atomic philosophy as stated by Lucretius. There
seems no doubt that Molière began and almost or quite
finished a translation of the *De Natura Rerum.* According
to a manuscript note of Trallage, published by M. Paul
Lacroix, the manuscript was sold by Molière's widow to a
bookseller. His philosophic studies left a deep mark on the
genius of Molière. In the *Jugement de Pluton sur les deux
parties des Nouveaux Dialogues des Morts* (1684), the verdict
is 'Que Molière ne parleroit point de Philosophie.' To
'talk philosophy' was a favourite exercise of his during his
life, and his ideas are indicated with sufficient clearness in
several of his plays. From his study of philosophy, too, he
gained his knowledge of the ways of contemporary pedants—
of Pancrase the Aristotelian ; of Marphorius the Cartesian ;
of Trissotin, 'qui s'attache pour l'ordre au Péripatétisme' ;
of Philaminte, who loves Platonism ; of Belise, who relishes
'les petits corps'; and Armande, who loves 'les Tourbillons.'
Grimarest has an amusing anecdote of a controversy in which
Molière, defending Descartes, chose a lay-brother of a begging
order for umpire, while Chapelle appealed to the same expert
in favour of Gassendi. His college education over, Molière
studied law, and there is even evidence (the evidence of tra-

dition, in Grimarest, and of Le Boulanger de Chalussay, the libellous author of a play called *Élomire Hypochondre*) to prove that he was actually called to the bar. More trustworthy is the passing remark in La Grange's short biography (1682), '*au sortir des écoles de droit*, il choisit la profession de comédien.' Before joining a troop of half-amateur comedians, however, Molière had some experience in his father's business. In 1637 his father had obtained for him the right to succeed to his own office as *valet tapissier de chambre du Roi.* The document is mentioned in the inventory of Molière's effects, taken after his death. When the king travelled, the *valet tapissier* went before him to arrange the furniture of the royal quarters. There is very good reason to believe that Molière accompanied Louis XIII to Provence as his *valet tapissier* in 1642. It is even not impossible that Molière was the young *valet de chambre* who concealed Cinq Mars just before his arrest at Narbonne, June 13, 1642. But this is part of the romance rather than of the history of Molière. Our next glimpse of the comedian we get in a document of January 6, 1643. Molière acknowledges the receipt of money due to him from his deceased mother's estate, and gives up his claim to succeed his father as *valet de chambre du Roi.* On December 28 of the same year we learn, again from documentary evidence, that Jean Baptiste Poquelin, with Joseph Béjard, Madeleine Béjard, Geneviève Béjard, and others, had hired a tennis-court, and fitted it up as a stage for dramatic performances. The company called themselves L'Illustre Théâtre, *illustre* being then almost a slang word, very freely employed by the writers of the period.

Molière passed the year 1644 in playing with, and helping to manage, the Théâtre Illustre. The company acted in various tennis-courts, with very little success. Molière was actually arrested by·the tradesman who supplied candles, and the company had to borrow money from one Aubrey to release their leader from the Grand Châtelet (August 13, 1645). The process of turning a tennis-court into a theatre was somewhat expensive, even though no seats were provided in the pit. The troupe was for a short time under the protection of the Duc d'Orléans, but his favours were not lucrative. The·

Duc de Guise, according to some verses printed in 1646, made Molière a present of his cast-off wardrobe. But costume was not enough to draw the public to the tennis-court theatre of the Croix Noire, and empty houses at last obliged the Théâtre Illustre to leave Paris at the end of 1646.

'Nul animal vivant n'entra dans nôtre salle,' says the author of the scurrilous play on Molière, *Élomire Hypochondre*. But at that time some dozen travelling companies found means to exist in the provinces, and Molière determined to play among the rural towns. The career of a strolling player is much the same at all times and in all countries. The *Roman Comique* of Scarron gives a vivid picture of the adventures and misadventures, the difficulty of transport, the queer cavalcade of horses, mules, and lumbering carts that drag the wardrobe and properties, the sudden metamorphosis of the tennis-court, where the balls have just been rattling, into a stage, the quarrels with local squires, the disturbed nights in crowded country inns, all the loves and wars of a troop on the march. Perrault tells us what the arrangements of the Theatre were in Molière's early time. Tapestries were hung round the stage, and entrances and exits were made by struggling through the heavy curtains, which often knocked off the hat of the comedian, or gave a strange cock to the helmet of a warrior or a god. The lights were candles stuck in tin sconces at the back and sides, but luxury sometimes went so far that a chandelier of four candles was suspended from the roof. At intervals the candles were let down by a rope and pulley, and any one within easy reach snuffed them with his fingers. A flute and tambour, or two fiddlers, supplied the music. The highest prices were paid for seats in the *dedans* (price of admission, fivepence) ; for the privilege of standing up in the pit twopence-halfpenny was the charge. The doors were opened at one o'clock, the curtain rose at two.

The nominal director of the Théâtre Illustre in the provinces was Du Fresne ; the most noted actors were Molière, the Béjards, and Du Parc, called Gros René. It is extremely difficult to follow exactly the line of march of the company. They played at Bordeaux, for example ; but the date of this occasion, when Molière (according to Montesquieu) failed in tragedy and was pelted, is variously given as 1644-45 (Trallage), 1647 (Loiseleur), 1648-58 (Lacroix). Doubtless the theatre prospered better anywhere than in Paris, where the streets were barricaded in these early days of the war of the Fronde. We find Molière at Nantes in 1648, at Fontenay-le-Compte, and in the spring of 1649 at Agen, at Toulouse, probably at Angoulême and Limoges. In January, 1650, they played at Narbonne, and between 1650 and 1653 Lyons was the headquarters of the troupe. In January, 1653, or perhaps 1655, Molière gave *L'Étourdi* at Lyons, the first of his finished pieces, as contrasted with the slight farces with which he generally diverted a country audience. It would be interesting to have the precise date of this piece, but La Grange (1682) says that 'in 1653 Molière went to Lyons, where he gave his first comedy, *L'Étourdi,*' while in his *Registre* La Grange enters the year as 1655. At Lyons De Brie and his wife, the famous Mlle. de Brie, entered the troupe, and Du Parc married Marquise de Gorla, better known as Mlle. du Parc. The libellous author of *La Fameuse Comédienne* reports that Molière's heart was the shuttlecock of the beautiful Du Parc and De Brie, and the tradition has a persistent life. Molière's own opinion of the ladies and men of his company may be read between the lines of his *Impromptu de Versailles.* In 1653 the Prince de Conti, after many military adventures, was residing at La Grange, near Pézénas, in Languedoc, and chance brought him into relations with his old schoolfellow Molière. Conti had for first gentleman of his bed-chamber the Abbé Daniel de Cosnac, whose memoirs now throw light for a moment on the fortunes of the wandering troupe. Cosnac engaged the company 'of Molière and of la Béjart'; but another company, that of Cormier, nearly intercepted the favour of the prince. Thanks to the resolution of Cosnac, Molière was given one chance of appearing on the private theatre of La Grange. The excellence of his acting, the splendour of the costumes, and the insistance of Cosnac, and of Sarrasin, Conti's secretary, gained the day for Molière, and a pension was assigned to his company (Cosnac,

Mémoires, i. 128 : Paris, 1852). In 1654, during the session of the Estates of Languedoc, Molière and his company played at Montpellier. Here Molière danced in a *ballet* (*Le Ballet des Incompatibles*), in which a number of men of rank took part, according to the fashion of the time. Molière's own *rôles* were those of the Poet and the Fishwife. The sport of the little piece is to introduce opposite characters, dancing and singing together. Silence dances with six women ; Truth with four courtiers ; Money with a Poet, and so forth. Whether the Ballet, or any parts of it, are by Molière, is still disputed (*La Jeunesse de Molière, Suivie du Ballet des Incompatibles*, P. Lacroix : Paris, 1858). In April, 1655, it is certain that the troupe was at Lyons, where they met and hospitably entertained a profligate buffoon, Charles d'Assoucy, who informs the ages that Molière kept open house, and *une table bien garnie*. November, 1655, found Molière at Pézénas, where the Estates of Languedoc were convened, and where local tradition points out the barber's chair in which the poet used to sit and study character. The longest of Molière's extant autographs is a receipt, dated at Pézénas, February 4, 1656, for 6000 *livres*, granted by the Estates of Languedoc. This year was notable for the earliest representation, at Béziers, of Molière's second finished comedy, the *Dépit Amoureux*. Conti now withdrew to Paris, and began to 'make his soul' as the Irish say. Almost his first act of penitence was to discard Molière's troupe (1657), which consequently found that the liberality of the Estates of Languedoc was dried up for ever. Conti's relations with Molière must have definitely closed long before 1666, when the now pious prince wrote a treatise against the stage, and especially charged his old schoolfellow with keeping a new school, a school of Atheism (*Traité de la Comédie*, p. 24 : Paris, MDCLXVI). Molière was now (1657) independent of princes and their favour. He went on a fresh circuit to Nîmes, Orange, and Avignon, where he met another old classmate, Chapelle, and also encountered the friend of his later life, the painter Mignard. After a later stay at Lyons, ending with a piece given for the benefit of the poor on February 27, 1658, Molière

passed to Grenoble, returned to Lyons, and is next found
in Rouen, where, we should have said, the Théâtre Illustre
had played in 1643. At Rouen Molière must have made or
renewed the acquaintance of Pierre and Thomas Corneille.
His company had played pieces by Corneille at Lyons and
elsewhere. The real business of the comedian in Rouen
was to prepare his return to Paris. 'After several secret
journeys thither he was fortunate enough to secure the
patronage of Monsieur, the king's only brother, who granted
him his protection, and permitted the company to take his
name, presenting them as his servants to the king and the
queen-mother' (Preface to La Grange's edition of 1682).
The troupe appeared for the first time before Louis XIV, in
a theatre arranged in the old Louvre (October 24, 1658).

Molière was now thirty-six years of age. He had gained
all the experience that fifteen years of practice could give.
He had seen men and cities, and noted all the humours of
rural and civic France. He was at the head of a company
which, as La Grange, his friend and comrade, says, 'sin-
cerely loved him.' He had the unlucrative patronage of
a great prince to back him, and the jealousy of all play-
wrights, and of the old theatres of the Hôtel de Bourgogne
and the Marais to contend against. In this struggle we
can follow him by aid of the *Registre* of La Grange (a brief
diary of receipts and payments), and by the help of notices
in the rhymed chronicles of Loret.

The first appearance of Molière before the king was all
but a failure. *Nicomède*, by the elder Corneille, was the
piece, and we may believe that the actors of the Hôtel de
Bourgogne, who were present, found much to criticise.
When the play was over, Molière came forward and asked
the king's permission to act 'one of the little pieces with
which he had been used to regale the provinces.' The
Docteur Amoureux, one of several slight comedies admitting
of much 'gag,' was then performed, and 'diverted as much
as it surprised the audience.' The king commanded that the
troupe should establish itself in Paris. The theatre assigned
to the company was a *salle* in the Petit Bourbon, in a line
with the present Rue du Louvre. Some Italian players

already occupied the house on Tuesdays, Fridays, and Sundays; the company of Molière played on the other days. The first piece played in the new house (Nov. 3, 1658) was *L'Étourdi*. La Grange says the comedy had a great success, producing seventy *pistoles* for each actor. The success is admitted even by the spiteful author of *Élomire Hypochondre* (Paris, 1670)—

'Je jouai l'Étourdi, qui fut une merveille.'

The success, however, is attributed to the farcical element in the play and the acting: this charge of *farceur* was the cuckoo cry of Molière's detractors. The original of *L'Étourdi* is the Italian comedy (1629) *L'Inavvertito*, by Nicolò Barbieri detto Beltrame; Molière pushed rather far his right to 'take his own wherever he found it.' Had he written nothing more original, the contemporary critic of the *Festin de Pierre* might have said, not untruly, that he only excelled in stealing pieces from the Italians. The piece is conventional: the stock characters of the prodigal son, the impudent valet, the old father occupy the stage. But the dialogue has amazing rapidity, and the vivacity of M. Coquelin in Mascarille still makes *L'Étourdi* a favourite on the stage, though it cannot be read with quite so much pleasure. The next piece, new in Paris, though not in the provinces, was the *Dépit Amoureux*. The play was not less successful than *L'Étourdi*. It has two parts, one an Italian *imbroglio*; the other, which alone keeps the stage, is the original work of Molière, though, of course, the idea of *amantium iræ* is as old as literature. 'Nothing so good,' says Mr. Saintsbury, 'had yet been seen on the French stage, as the quarrels and reconciliations of the quartette of master, mistress, valet, and soubrette.' Even the hostile Le Boulanger de Chalussay (*Élomire Hypochondre*) admits that the audience was much of this opinion—

'Et de tous les côtés chacun cria tout haut
"C'est là faire et jouer les pièces comme il faut."'

The same praise was given, perhaps even more deservedly,

to *Les Precieuses Ridicules* (November 18, 1659). Doubts have been raised as to whether this famous piece, the first true comic satire of contemporary foibles on the French stage, was a new play. La Grange calls it *pièce nouvelle* in his *Registre*; but, as he enters it as the third *pièce nouvelle*, he may only mean that, like *L'Étourdi*, it was new to Paris. The abridged life of 1682, produced under La Grange's care, and probably written by Marcel the actor, says the *Précieuses* was 'made' in 1659. Molière's next piece was less important, and more purely farcical, *Sganarelle; ou le Cocu Imaginaire* (May 28, 1660). The public taste preferred a work of this light nature, and *Sganarelle* was played every year as long as Molière lived. The play was pirated by a man who pretended to have retained all the words in his memory. The counterfeit copy was published by Ribou, a double injury to Molière, as, once printed, any company might act the play. With his habitual good-nature, Molière not only allowed Ribou to publish later works of his, but actually lent money to that publisher (Soulié, *Recherches,* p. 287).

On October 11, 1660, the Théâtre du Petit Bourbon was demolished by the Superintendent of Works, without notice given to the company. The king gave Molière the *salle du Palais Royal*, but the machinery of the old theatre was maliciously destroyed. Meanwhile the older companies of the Marais and the Hôtel de Bourgogne attempted to lure away Molière's troupe; but, as La Grange declares (*Registre,* p. 26), 'all the actors loved their chief, who united to extraordinary genius an honourable character and charming manner, which compelled them all to protest that they would never leave him, but always share his fortunes.' While the new theatre was being put in order, the company played in the houses of the great, and before the king at the Louvre. In their new house (originally built by Richelieu) Molière began to play on January 20, 1661. Molière now gratified his rivals by a failure. *Don Garcie de Navarre* had long lain among his papers, a heavy tragi-comedy, which was first represented on February 4, 1661. Either Molière was a poor actor outside comedy, or his manner was not sufficiently 'stagy' and, as he says, 'demoniac,' for the taste of the day. His opponents were determined that he could not act in tragi-comedy, and he, in turn, burlesqued their pretentious and exaggerated manner in a later piece. In the *Précieuses* (sc. xi.) Molière had already rallied 'les grands comédiens' of the Hôtel de Bourgogne. 'Les autres,' he makes Mascarille say about his own troupe, 'sont des ignorants qui récitent comme l'on parle, ils ne savent pas faire ronfler les vers.' All this was likely to irritate the *grands comédiens* and their friends, who avenged themselves on that unfortunate jealous prince, Don Garcie de Navarre. The subject of this unsuccessful drama is one of many examples which show how Molière's mind was engaged with the serious or comic aspects of jealousy, a passion which he had soon cause to know most intimately. Meantime the existing life of the stage went on, and the doorkeeper of the Théâtre St. Germain was wounded by some revellers who tried to thrust their way into the house (La Grange, *Registre*). A year later, an Italian actor was stabbed in front of Molière's house, where he had sought to take shelter (Campardon, *Nouvelles Pièces*, p. 20). To these dangers actors were peculiarly subject : Molière himself was frequently threatened by the marquises and others whom he ridiculed on the stage, and there even seems reason to believe that there is some truth in the story of the angry marquis who rubbed the poet's head against his buttons, thereby cutting his face severely. The story comes late (1725) into his biography, but is supported by a passage in the contemporary play, *Zélinde* (Paris, 1663, scene viii.). Before Easter, Molière asked for two shares in the profits of his company, one for himself, and one for his wife, if he married (La Grange). That fatal step was already contemplated. On June 24 he brought out for the first time *L'École des Maris.* The general idea of the piece is as old as Menander, and Molière was promptly accused of pilfering from the *Adelphi* of Terence. One of the *ficelles* of the comedy is borrowed from a story as old, at least, as Boccaccio, and still amusing in a novel by Charles de Bernard. It is significant of Molière's talent that the grotesque and

baffled paternal wooer, Sganarelle, like several other butts
in Molière's comedy, does to a certain extent win our
sympathy and pity as well as our laughter. The next new
piece was *Les Fascheux*, a *comédie-ballet*, the Comedy of
Bores, played before the king at Fouquet's house at Vaux
le Vicomte (August 15–20, 1661). The comedians, without
knowing it, were perhaps the real *Fascheux* on this occasion,
for Fouquet was absorbed in the schemes of his insatiable
ambition (*Quo non ascendam?* says his motto), and the king
was organizing the arrest and fall of Fouquet, his rival in
the affections of La Vallière. The author of the prologue to
Les Fascheux, Pellisson, a friend of Fouquet's, was arrested
along with the Superintendent of Finance. Pellisson's prologue and name were retained in later editions. In the
dedication to the king, Molière says that Louis suggested
one scene (that of the Sportsman), and in another place
mentions that the piece was written, rehearsed, and played
in a fortnight. The fundamental idea of the play, the inter-
ruptions by bores, is suggested by a satire of Régnier's, and
that by a satire of Horace. Perhaps it may have been the
acknowledged hints of the king which made gossips declare
that Molière habitually worked up notes and *mémoires* given
him by persons of quality (*Nouvelles Nouvelles*, 1663).

In February, 1662, Molière married Armande Béjard.
The date of the marriage is difficult to determine, and it
must be infinitely harder to discover the truth as to the
conduct of Madame Molière. The abominable assertions
of the anonymous libel, *Les Intrigues de Molière et celles de
sa Femme; ou, la Fameuse Comédienne* (1688), have found
their way into tradition, and are accepted by many biographers. But M. Livet and M. Bazin have proved that
the alleged lovers of Madame Molière were actually absent
from France, or from the court, at the time when they are
reported, in the libel, to have conquered her heart. A
conversation between Chapelle and Molière, in which the
comedian is made to tell the story of his wrongs, is plainly
a mere fiction, and is answered in Grimarest by another
dialogue between Molière and Rohault, in which Molière
only complains of a jealousy which he knows to be un-

founded. It is noticed, too, that the contemporary assailants of Molière counted him among jealous, but not among deceived, husbands. A hideous accusation brought by the actor Montfleury, Louis XIV answered merely by becoming the godfather of Molière's child. The king, indeed, was a firm friend of the actor, and, when Molière was accused of impiety on the production of *Don Juan* (1665), Louis gave him a pension. It is generally thought that Molière drew his wife's portrait in *Le Bourgeois Gentilhomme,* acte iii. sc. ix., 'elle est capricieuse, mais on souffre tout des Belles[1].'

From 1662 onwards, Molière suffered the increasing hatred of his rival actors. La Grange mentions the visit of Floridor and Montfleury to the queen-mother, and their attempt to obtain equal favour—'la troupe de Molière leur donnant beaucoup de jalouzie' (August 12, 1662). On December 26 was played for the first time the admirable *École des Femmes,* which provoked a literary war, and caused a shower of 'paper bullets of the brain.' The innocence of Agnes was called indecency; the sermon of Arnolphe was a deliberate attack on Christian mysteries.

In all those quarrels the influence of Corneille was opposed to Molière, while his cause was espoused by Boileau, a useful ally, when 'les comédiens et les auteurs, depuis le cèdre [Corneille?] jusqu'à l'hysope, sont diablement animés contre lui' (*Impromptu de Versailles,* scène v.).

Molière's next piece was *Le Mariage Forcé* (February 15, 1664), a farce with a ballet. The comic character of the reluctant bridegroom wins sympathy, or rather pity, as well as laughter. From the end of April till May 22 the troupe was at Versailles, among the picturesque pleasures of that great festival of the king's. The *Princesse d'Élide* was acted for the first time, and the first three acts of *Tartuffe* were given. Molière's natural hatred of hypocrisy had not been diminished by the charges of blasphemy which were showered on him after the *École des Femmes. Tartuffe*

---

[1] The problems suggested by Molière's marriage are discussed in the *Encyclopaedia Britannica,* under MOLIÈRE.

made enemies everywhere. Jansenists and Jesuits, like the
two marquises·in *L'Impromptu de Versailles*, each thought
the others were aimed at. Five years passed before Molière
got permission to play the whole piece in public. In the
interval it was acted before Madame Condé, before the
Legate, and was frequently read by Molière in private houses.
The *Gazette* of May 17, 1664 (a paper hostile to Molière)
says that the king thought the piece inimical to religion.
Louis was not at that time on good terms with the *dévots*,
whom his amours scandalized ; but, not impossibly, the
queen-mother (then suffering from her fatal malady) disliked
the play. A most violent attack on Molière, 'that demon
clad in human flesh,' was written by one Pierre Roullé (*Le
Roy Glorieux au Monde*: Paris, 1664). This fierce pamphlet
was suppressed, but the king's own copy, in red morocco,
with the royal arms, remains to testify to the bigotry of the
author, who was curé of Saint Barthélemy. According to
Roullé, Molière deserved to be sent through earthly to
eternal fires. The play was prohibited, as we have seen ;
but in August 1665 the king adopted Molière's troupe as his
servants, and gave them the title of *Troupe du Roy*. This,
however, did not cause Molière to relax his efforts to obtain
permission for *Tartuffe* (or *Tartufe*, or *Tartufle*, as it was
variously spelled), and his perseverance was at length successful. That his thoughts were busy with contemporary
hypocrisy is proved by certain scenes in one of his greatest
pieces, the *Festin de Pierre*, or *Don Juan* (February 15,
1665). The legend of *Don Juan* was already familiar on
the Spanish, Italian, and French stages. Molière made it a
new thing, terrible and romantic in its portrait of *un grand
seigneur mauvais homme*, modern in its suggested substitution of *l'humanité* for religion, comic, even among his
comedies, by the mirthful character of Sganarelle. The piece
filled the theatre, but was stopped, probably by authority,
after Easter. It was not printed by Molière, and, even in
1682, the publication of the full text was not permitted.
Happily, the copy of De la Regnie, the chief of the police,
escaped obliterations, and gave us the full scene of Don Juan
and the Beggar. The piece provoked a virulent criticism

(*Observations sur le Festin de Pierre*, 1665). It is allowed that Molière has some farcical talent, and is not unskilled as a plagiarist, but he 'attacks the interests of Heaven,' 'keeps a school of infidelity,' 'insults the king,' 'corrupts virtue,' 'offends the queen-mother,' and so forth. Two replies were published; one of them is by some critics believed to show traces of the hand of Molière. The king's answer, as has been shown, was to adopt Molière's company as his servants, and to pension them. *L'Amour Médecin*, a light comedy, appeared September 22, 1665. In this piece Molière, for the second time, attacked physicians. In December there was a quarrel with Racine about his play of *Alexandre*, which he treacherously transferred to L'Hôtel de Bourgogne. June 4, 1666 saw the first representation of that famous play, *Le Misanthrope* (*ou L'Atrabiliaire Amoureux*, as the original second title ran). This piece, perhaps the masterpiece of Molière, was more successful with the critics, with the court, and with posterity, than with the public. The rival comedians called it 'a new style of comedy,' and so it was. The eternal passions and sentiments of human nature, modified by the influence of the utmost refinement of civilization, were the matter of the piece. The school for scandal kept by Célimène, with its hasty judgments on all characters, gave the artist a wide canvas. The perpetual strife between the sensible optimism of a kindly man of the world (Philinte) and the *sæva indignatio* of a noble nature soured (Alceste) supplies the intellectual action. The humours of the joyously severe Célimène and of her court, especially of that deathless minor poet Oronte, provide the lighter comedy. Boileau, Lessing, Goethe have combined to give this piece the highest rank even among the comedies of Molière. As to the 'keys' to the characters, and the guesses about the original from whom Alceste was drawn, they are as valueless as other contemporary tattle.   .

A briefer summary must be given of the remaining years of the life of Molière. The attractions of *Le Misanthrope* were reinforced (August 6) by those of the *Médecin Malgré Lui*, an amusing farce founded on an old *fabliau*. In December the court and the comedians went to Saint Germain,

where, among other diversions, the play called *Mélicerte*,
La Pastorale Comique (of which Molière is said to have destroyed the MS.), and the charming little piece *Le Sicilien*
were performed. A cold and fatigue seem to have injured
the health of Molière, and we now hear of the consumptive
tendency, which was cruelly ridiculed in *Élomire Hypochondre*. Molière was doubtless obliged to see too much of
the distracted or pedantic physicians of an age when medicine was the battlefield of tradition, superstition, and nascent
chemical science. On April 17, 1667, Robinet, the rhyming
gazetteer, says that the life of Molière was thought to be in
danger. On June 10, however, he played in *Le Sicilien*
before the town. In the earlier months of 1667 Louis XIV
was with the army in Flanders. There were embassies sent
from the comedy to the camp, and on August 5 it was apparent that Molière had overcome the royal scruples. *Tartuffe* was played, but Lamoignon stopped it after the first
night. La Grange and La Torillière hastened to the camp,
and got the king's promise that he would reconsider the
matter on his return. Molière's next piece (January 13, 1668)
was *Amphitryon*, a free, a very free adaptation from Plautus,
who then seems to have engaged his attention, for not long
afterwards he again borrowed from the ancient writer in
L'Avare. There is a controversy as to whether *Amphitryon*
was meant to ridicule M. de Montespan, the husband of the
new mistress of Louis XIV. Michelet has a kind of romance
based on this probably groundless hypothesis. The king
still saw the piece occasionally, after he had purged himself
and forsworn sack, under Madame de Maintenon, and
probably neither he nor that devout lady detected any per-
sonal references in the coarse and witty comedy. As usual,
Molière was accused of plagiarising, this time from Rotrou,
who had also imitated Plautus. The next play was the immortal *George Dandin* (July 10), first played at a festival
at Versailles. The piece was a rapid palimpsest on the
ground of one of his old farces, but the addition of those
typical members of a county family, the De Sotenville, raises
the work from farce to satiric comedy. The story is borrowed
from Boccaccio, but is of unknown age, and always new—

Adolphus Crosbie in *The Small House at Allington* being a kind of modern George Dandin. Though the sad fortunes of this peasant with social ambition do not fail to make us pity him somewhat, it is being too refined to regard *George Dandin* as a comedy with a concealed tragic intention. Molière must have been at work on *L'Avare* before *George Dandin* appeared, for the new comedy after Plautus was first acted on September 9. There is a tradition that the piece almost failed ; but if unpopular in the first year of its production, it certainly gained favour before the death of its author. *M. de Pourceaugnac* (September 17, 1669) was first acted at Chambord, for the amusement of the king. It is a rattling farce. The physicians, as usual, bore the brunt of Molière's raillery, some of which is still applicable. Earlier in 1669 (February 5) *Tartuffe* was played at last with extraordinary success. *Les Amants Magnifiques*, a comedy-ballet, was acted first at Saint Germain (February 10, 1670). The king might have been expected to dance in the ballet, but, from Racine's *Britannicus* (December 13, 1669), the majestical monarch learned that Nero was blamed for exhibitions of this kind, and he did not wish to out-Nero Nero. Astrology this time took the place of Medicine as a butt, but the satire has become obsolete, except, perhaps, in Turkey, where astrology is still a power. The *Bourgeois Gentilhomme*, too familiar to require analysis, was first played on October 23, 1670. The lively *Fourberies de Scapin* 'saw the footlights' (if footlights there were) on May 24, 1671, and on May 7 we read in La Grange, 'Les Repetitions de Spsyche ont commancé.' La Grange says the theatre was newly decorated and fitted with machines. A 'concert of twelve violins' was also provided, the company being resolute to have everything handsome about them. New singers were introduced, who did not refuse to sing, unmasked, on the stage. Quinault composed the words for the music, which was by Lulli ; Molière and Pierre Corneille collaborated in the dialogue of this magnificent opera, the name of which (*Psyche*) La Grange eventually learned how to spell. The *Comtesse d'Escarbagnas* (February 2, 1672) was another piece for the amusement of the court, and made part of an entertainment called *Le Ballet des*

Ballets. In this play, a study of provincial manners, Molière attacked the financiers of the time in the person of M. Harpin. The comedy has little importance compared with *Les Femmes Savantes* (February 11), a severer *Précieuses,* in which are satirized the vanity and affectation of sciolists, pedants, and the women who admire them. The satire is never out of date, and finds its modern form in *Le Monde où l'on s'ennuie,* by M. Pailleron. On February 17 Madeleine Béjard died, and was buried at St. Paul. She did not go long before her old friend or lover, Molière. His *Mariage Forcé,* founded, perhaps, on a famous anecdote of De Grammont, was played on July 8. On August 7 La Grange notes that Molière was indisposed, and there was no comedy. Molière's son died on October 11. On November 22 the preparations for the *Malade Imaginaire* were begun. On February 10, 1673, the piece was acted for the first time. What occurred on February 17 we translate from the *Registre* of La Grange :—

'This same day, about ten o'clock at night, after the comedy, Monsieur de Molière died in his house, Rue de Richelieu. He had played the part of the said Malade, suffering much from cold and in-flammation, which caused a violent cough. In the violence of the cough he burst a vessel in his body, and did not live more than half an hour or three quarters after the bursting of the vessel. His body is buried at St. Joseph's, parish of St. Eustache. There is a grave-stone raised about a foot above the ground.'

Molière's funeral is thus described in a letter, said to be by an eye-witness, discovered by M. Benjamin Fillon :—

'Tuesday, February 21, about nine in the evening, was buried Jean Baptiste Poquelin Molière, *tapissier valet de chambre,* and a famous actor. There was no procession, except three ecclesiastics; four priests bore the body in a wooden bier covered with a pall, six chil-dren in blue carried candles in silver holders, and there were lackeys with burning torches of wax. The body . . . was taken to St. Joseph's churchyard, and buried at the foot of the cross. There was a great crowd, and some twelve hundred livres were distributed among the poor. The archbishop had given orders that Molière should be interred without any ceremony, and had even forbidden the clergy of the diocese to do any service for him. Nevertheless a number of masses were ordered to be said for the deceased.'

C

When an attempt was made to exhume the body of Molière in 1792, the wrong tomb appears to have been opened. Unknown is the grave of Molière.

Molière, according to Mlle. Poisson, who had seen him in her extreme youth, was 'neither too stout nor too thin, tall rather than short; he had a noble carriage, a good leg, walked slowly, and had a very serious expression. His nose was thick, his mouth large, with thick lips, his complexion brown, his eyebrows black and strongly marked, and it was his way of moving these that gave him his comic expression on the stage.' 'His eyes seemed to search the deeps of men's hearts,' says the author of *Zélinde*. The inventories printed by M. Soulié prove that Molière was fond of rich dress, splendid furniture, and old books. The charm of his conversation is attested by the names of his friends, who were all the wits of the age, and the greater their genius the greater their love of Molière. As an actor, friends and enemies agreed in recognizing him as most successful in comedy. His ideas of tragic declamation were in advance of his time, for he set his face against the prevalent habit of ranting. His private character was remarkable for gentleness, probity, generosity, and delicacy, qualities attested not only by anecdotes but by the evidence of documents. He is probably (as Menander is lost) the greatest of all comic writers within the limits of social and refined as distinguished from romantic comedy, like that of Shakespeare, and from political comedy, like that of Aristophanes. He has the humour which is but a sense of the true value of life, and now takes the form of the most vivacious wit, and the keenest observation, now of melancholy, and pity, and wonder, at the fortunes of mortal men. In the literature of France his is the greatest name, and in the literature of the modern drama, the greatest after that of Shakespeare. Besides his contemplative genius he possessed an unerring knowledge of the theatre, the knowledge of a great actor and a great manager, and hence his plays can never cease to hold the stage, and to charm, if possible, even more in the performance than in the reading.

II. THE PROGRESS OF FRENCH COMEDY.

THE history of French comedy is of peculiar importance in reference to the progress of the drama in France, though its stages have not been illustrated by any such striking changes, or, with the exception of Molière, by any names of such importance as those which illustrate the annals of French tragedy. A hasty reader might decide that there is nothing in common between the tragedy of Racine and of Hugo : a reader who is not at all hasty might come to the same decision between the tragedy of Racine and of the mystery writers. But from the very earliest farces, indeed from the *Jeu de Robin et Marion* and the *Jeu de la Feuillie* of Adam de la Halle in the thirteenth century, the progress of French comedy is constant and uninterrupted. The two great turning-points of the history of tragedy—the reform of the Pléïade and the further reform of the mid-seventeenth century—have nothing to correspond to them on the comic side. No two things can well be more different than a tragedy of Jodelle and a mystery of his chief immediate predecessor Chevallet. But Jodelle's comedy *Eugène*, though it shows the influence of Terence, is rather an improved version of the old farces than a new style, and Molière's great comedies are only separated from his own *Jalousie du Barbouillé* and *Médecin Volant* by improvements of degree not of kind. It is therefore unnecessary to divide an essay on French comedy, to whatever author it may have immediate reference. From Adam de la Halle to Sardou the history of the French comedy is as continuous as the history of the English Parliament from Simon de Montfort to Lord Beaconsfield.

Comedy, however, though it has a more continuous, has a less early history than tragedy. We can trace tragedies, or at least 'histories' (in the sense in which the word is used in reference to the early English drama), to the eleventh century, if not earlier : it is not until the thirteenth that comedy assumes an independent form, though there are

C 2

comic interludes in serious plays before that date. This is in accordance with general experience, and still more in accordance with the fact that the early French drama was entirely under ecclesiastical influence. There was nothing Puritanic in the mediaeval Church, but it naturally did not go out of its way to invent or favour purely secular amusements. There are comic scenes in more than one early mystery (indeed, it is rather the exception to find one without such); but no comedy pure and simple appears till the third quarter of the thirteenth century. Adam de la Halle, a native of Arras, of whose history little is known, about that date produced two plays which in different ways deserve the title, the dramatised pastourelle of *Robin et Marion* and the already mentioned *Jeu de la Feuillie*. The pastourelle proper is a peculiar form of ballad-romance which was extremely popular in the middle ages, and which, with infinite variety of detail, has an almost invariable subject. A fair shepherdess who has a rustic lover meets the eye of a knight who passes by, is courted by him, and, as the case may be, jilts or is faithful to her swain. The dramatic capabilities of the story are obvious, but though the pastourelle as a poem had been popular long before Adam's days, there is no evidence that any one thought of working it out dramatically before him. In *Robin et Marion* the characters of the shepherdess (who is in this case a faithful shepherdess), the lover, and the knight all appear, act and speak in their own persons: the remainder of the *dramatis personae* being provided by the rustic neighbours of the pair who help in rescuing Marion from the knight. The piece is of course slight, and so much of the dialogue is in lyrical form that it is rather entitled to the name of a comic opera than of a comedy. But the important point about it is that it is entirely secular in subject and characters, that it is purely comic, and that its plot, slight as it is, is substantive and sufficiently worked out. The *Jeu de la Feuillie* (*feuillie* or *feuillée* = booth or tabernacle of boughs) is a more ambitious and complex performance, but by no means so complete and perfect in form. The poet himself, his father, and some of his friends appear in it, and, so far as it can be

said to have a plot, this plot consists in the revelation of
Adam's own life (whence the piece is sometimes called the
Jeu Adam) mixed with a good deal of illnatured satire on
his wife, father, and friends. There is thus little systematic
action, and what there is is confused still further by a
strange interlude of fictitious persons who have nothing to do
with the real actors. Still the piece is in the first place entirely secular, and in the second purely comic—two circumstances which give it equal importance with *Robin et Marion*
in history. It has sometimes been sought to associate
with these other early pieces which have the form of *débats*
—verse-dialogues—but most of these latter have nothing properly dramatic about them. On the other hand, rude as they
are, the two pieces just discussed are in every sense comedy
proper. But by an accident familiar to students of mediaeval
literature they seem to have found few or no imitators. The
fourteenth century passes unillumined by a single French
comedy, and the dramatic outburst of the fifteenth belongs
chiefly to its latest years. At this time, however, comedy
began to be popular. Of the four varieties of late mediaeval
drama in France—mystery, morality, *sotie*, and farce—the
last three belong to comedy. The morality is a comedy
with a purpose, the *sotie* a political comedy, the farce a
comedy pure and simple. The morality and the *sotie* con-
tribute less to the main stream of comic progress than the
farce. Not only did the moral purpose of the first and the
political purpose of the second interfere with them, but each
was, according to a survival of mediaeval fashions, burdened
with formal peculiarities which were unfavourable to its
development. The morality, as its name almost implies, had
to a great extent abstract personifications of moral qualities
for its characters; and thus allegorising, the bane of the
later mediaeval literature, affected it very strongly. The
sotie was still more artificial, the parts being played somewhat like those of the Italian *Commedia dell' Arte* by a
set of stock characters composing the supposed court of
the Prince des Sots; but the farce was subject to no such
restrictions, and (in an immature and rude form of course)
it deserves already the description of *la vraie comédie*. It

admitted of the widest licence of arrangement. Sometimes indeed there was only one character, in which case it was properly called a monologue. There were never very many, nor was the piece ever of much length, so that it rarely admitted of more than a single situation. But these situations, which, as might be expected, belong for the most part to the region of low comedy, not to say the broadest farce, are often treated with an adroitness which foreshows the remarkable dramatic achievements of the language. A plot to get a dinner gratis, to outwit a husband or a father, to gull a tradesman, to play a practical joke, is the staple of most of these pieces ; and the action is very often carried off very smartly and well, not without appropriate diction, and showing occasionally, within the somewhat narrow limits allowed, lively pictures of manners, and even an attempt at character-drawing. As on the whole the subjects of the farces partook of the general and obvious commonplaces of comedy, they lent themselves well enough to development and adaptation under the influence of the Terentian drama when the Renaissance made the study of classical literature fashionable.

The style of these farces themselves had already fastened strongly on the French taste, and it suffered, as has been said, very little and gained much from the all-reforming energy of the Pléïade. *Eugène*, which enjoys the title of being the first French regular comedy, and which was written and represented simultaneously with the first French tragedy *Cléopâtre*, is much more advanced in scheme and scale than the earlier farces. It has a succession of situations, not a single one ; it aims at some display of individual as well as typical character. But it is after all only a farce complex instead of a farce simple. The main difference is the regular division into acts and scenes, and the greater complexity of action which is due to a following of the regular classical comedy. There is a double plot with minor characters who have something like individuality, and the difference may perhaps best be expressed by saying that the play gives a complete story and not merely a chapter of a story. But *Eugène* is, like the farces, written

in octosyllabic lines, a metre insufficient for theatrical dialogue. The example was taken up by Jodelle's followers
Jacques Grévin wrote two comedies, *Les Esbahis* and *La
Trésorière*, which are improvements on Jodelle; Rémy
Belleau, one of the chiefs of the Pléïade, produced *La Re-
connue*, which is perhaps a still greater improvement; Baïf,
another important member of the group of seven, adapted
the *Miles Gloriosus* in his *Taillebras*. But neither dared
to discard the inconvenient and cramping octosyllable.
Some of their contemporaries were bolder, and threw the
dialogue into prose, which at once afforded far greater ease,
and in which, notwithstanding a certain relapse into deca-
syllabics or Alexandrines of an easier and less elaborate
kind than that used in tragedy, all the best comedies in
French have been written, with rare exceptions, for the last
three centuries. The chief of these innovators, and indeed
the most remarkable name in French comedy before Molière, was Pierre Larivey, an Italian by extraction, who was
born in 1540, and survived till the seventeenth century was
in its teens. Larivey is in one sense one of the most, and
in another one of the least, original of writers. Of the
twelve comedies which he wrote, nine of which we possess,
it would appear that every one had an Italian origin, while
most of them were imitated by their Italian authors from
Plautus and Terence. But Larivey adapted in the freest
possible fashion, and wrote his adaptations in French of
very considerable excellence for his time, besides displaying
no little stage knack. Molière borrowed something from
him directly, and was indirectly still more indebted to him
for advancing the general conception of French comedy by
complicating the plot, making the action brisk and lively,
and accustoming the spectators to demand smart 'humours'
and dialogue.

After Larivey, however, no very great advance was made,
with the exception of the comic work of Corneille, until
Molière himself, nearly half a century later, came to his
period of flourishing. The first half of the seventeenth century, though it witnessed a considerable amount of experi-
mentation in comic work, produced little that is of much

permanent interest. The old farces apparently continued
to be acted, and new ones of the same kind to be written
by the poets who were attached to every strolling company
of actors. Adapters, of whom Alexandre Hardy was the
chief, transferred many Spanish and Italian plays to the
French boards. Curious experiments were tried, such as
the writing of a comedy composed entirely of popular songs
or tags from them. Most of the tragedians of the time
wrote comedies, and Corneille's, even before the *Menteur*,
have decided merit and interest. The *Pédant Joué* of Cyrano de Bergerac gave Molière something to borrow, and
Paul Scarron was a dramatist of not a little popularity and
of some power. So also Quinault, Boursault, and Montfleury—contemporaries of the great comic writer—showed,
as the lesser contemporaries of great writers generally do
show, that genius is not the complete, independent, self-
caused and self-centred thing that uncritical critics would
sometimes have it to be. But in almost all comedies before
Molière, and in most written by other men during his life,
the reader feels that he is in presence of men who do
not distinctly know what they are aiming at, and who are
still unsure of their artillery. The dramatic construction is
faulty, the action lags, the comic motives are extravagant
or indecorous, the characters are improbable or unamusing,
the whole play lacks that direct and evident connection with
human life which is necessary in comedy. Even the first
two plays of Molière are in some sort liable to these ob-
jections, and the first two plays of Molière are far superior
to everything before them, with the exception of *Le Menteur*.

It is, however, still noticeable how little the general
scheme, as distinguished from the execution of French
comedy, is changed. A new influence is indeed brought
in to supplement the Latin, and the Italian-Spanish intrigue
comedies have their effect on the contemporaries of Corneille. The result appears in *Mélite*, still more in *Le Menteur*, but these various influences are conditioned by the fact
that comedy of all nations and languages is after all very
much the same. Aristophanes, Shakespeare, Molière, Plautus, had idiosyncrasies at least as different as Aeschylus,

Shakespeare, Corneille, Seneca. But what principally strikes the reader in comparing *Prometheus, Othello, Cinna, Octavia,* are differences : what principally strikes him in reading *The Birds, As You Like It, Les Précieuses Ridicules,* the *Mostellaria,* are resemblances. Here, at least, there is some proof that man is really and not merely in scholastic imagination a 'laughing animal.' But what is most remarkable in connection with the present subject is that Molière not merely follows his leaders but distinctly harks back in his following of them. The two existing examples of his earlier work, and the titles of the rest of that work, clearly show that for many years he wrote farces pure and simple—farces hardly changed in general plan between the middle of the fifteenth century and the middle of the seventeenth. When he took to a more serious style of composition he passed rapidly through the stages which French comedy had traversed since the time of his earlier models. Italian and Spanish models show themselves clearly in *L'Étourdi* and *Le Dépit Amoureux,* and when, following Corneille, he entered on true comedy with *Les Précieuses Ridicules,* only improvement (in the sense of studying the life rather than academic copies) not innovation (in the sense of substituting a new form for an old one) resulted. It may properly be asked at this point in what this general resemblance consists? The question is not very difficult to answer. In French comedy, as in all French comic literature, fidelity to nature has entirely the better of the close adherence to forms and types which obtained in many other departments of letters in France. There is this adherence to types even in comedy; and it is remarkable that despite all the genius and all the observation of Molière it receives some countenance from him. But when we contrast French comedy with any other comedy, or French comedy with any other department, save the modern novel, of French literature, it is in comparison conspicuously absent from the very first to the very last. The French comedy writer is freer from rules of any kind than any of his craftsfellows. He may take his comic situation and work it out as he likes, at the length that he likes, and with the conditions that he likes. He is not bound to prose or to verse. No unities torment him. He may have one act and a score of scenes, three acts and half a dozen scenes in each, five acts and any number of scenes he likes. His characters are unrestricted in number, and almost unrestricted in behaviour and diction. No *style noble* weighs on him, no Horatian theories of doing the action off the stage, no notion of the decorum of the Theatre. He is always able, whether he is a farce-writer of the fifteenth century dramatising a single rough or indecorous situation, or Molière in the seventeenth constructing complete and immortal criticisms of life, or M. Sardou and M. Feuillet in the nineteenth painting ephemeral manners—to shape his treatment to his subject, and not forced to shape his subject to his treatment. In short, the likeness which has been spoken of is the likeness that is sure to exist whenever men of any age or country allow themselves to be guided by nature.

Speaking roughly, it was in teaching his brethren, the French comic dramatists, to give themselves up to the guidance of nature more thoroughly than they had dared to do, and in raising the drama from the position of copying mere humours and stock subjects, that Molière achieved his greatest success. As we have endeavoured to point out in the preceding pages, the mere formal changes which he made—like the formal changes which all his predecessors had made on the simple original farce—were of very small account. It was by the alteration of the spirit and style of the drama, and by increasing the literary merit of its text—a matter in which up to his time comedy had been decidedly behind tragedy—that he mainly influenced the stage ; and, as in all such cases, the influence was exercised once for all. It was nearly impossible for the most arrant dunce to write so bad a comedy after Molière as men often of great talent and even genius had constantly written before him. Moreover, the great success of his plays raised the reputation as well as the literary standards of the comic dramatist, created an additional demand for comedy, and thus led to the subdivision of it into different kinds, with special apparatus for representing them. For about a hundred years after Molière's *début* comedy was represented in Paris (not always uninterruptedly in every case) by four different theatres, each of which had a special kind of drama. There was the Comédie Française, the successor of Molière's own company, which played mainly what would be called in English legitimate comedy. There was the Comédie Italienne, which, after being a visitor at the French capital, established itself there permanently in the eighteenth century, and played a peculiar variety of the same kind of dramas as the Comédie Française, adjusted more or less to the stock characters of the Italian comedy proper. There was the Opéra Comique, which explains itself, and which became popular when the originally Italian model of the musical drama (first established by Quinault as a writer of words and Lulli as a composer of music) had adjusted itself to French tastes. Lastly, there were the minor theatres— tolerated during the great fairs of St. Germain and St. Laurent, but at other times leading a rather precarious existence—which chiefly acted short pieces partaking of the comic operetta and the farce, and known generally at a later date under the title of *Vaudeville*. These three last-named varieties have somewhat less to do with literature proper than the first, but they all afforded employment to writers of eminence, and the Vaudeville has in one form or another held its ground not much altered till the present day. It was written in great numbers by Lesage, by Piron, by Collé, and other wits of the eighteenth century, and it was always extremely popular. Some of the expedients to which the jealousy of the regular actors reduced the Vaudevillistes were very curious—for instance, a piece was occasionally acted entirely in dumb show: the songs (*couplets*) which formed its libretto being successively displayed on large placards for the audience to sing. But it is impossible to enter into these details here; and the opera proper, where music rather than acting was the staple of the entertainment, also escapes us. The Italian Theatre had at least one very distinguished writer in Marivaux, but its pieces, except with regard to the already mentioned adaptation of the cast, are in most cases hardly distinguishable from those of the

Comédie Française. These latter continued till the middle of the eighteenth century, and with some modifications till the first quarter of the nineteenth, to be closely modelled upon Molière; and a short sketch may now be given of the principal authors who distinguished themselves therein. This sketch may conveniently extend without a break to the romantic revival, the partial change in the middle of the eighteenth century being returned to as a preliminary of the romantic revival itself, which indeed was less marked in regard to comedy than in regard to tragedy.

The excellence of Molière's work, the clearness with which he pointed out the way, and the great popularity of his drama, raised many imitators and followers when his own short and brilliant course was run. The greatest and one of the earliest of these was Regnard—one of the few members of the youngest generation in the 'Siècle de Louis Quatorze' who had the good fortune to secure the capricious and morose judgment of Boileau in his favour. Had Regnard lived a century later he might have been a French Byron; but in his days romantic adventure was not a path to popularity, nor did men who enjoyed to the full all the good things of this world think it necessary to bemoan themselves for the fact of their having enjoyed them. Regnard's plays were closely modelled on Molière, and in *Le Joueur, Le Légataire*, and others, he came very near to his master. In their turn Dufresny and Dancourt came nearest to Regnard, if bulk of production and general excellence are to be taken into account; but the joint authors Brueys and Palaprat, who modernised *L'Avocat Pathelin* (one of the best farces, and thanks to them incomparably the best known of the fifteenth century) produced in that and in *Le Grondeur* perhaps the best plays next to Regnard's of the immediate Molièresque tradition. All these authors, however, and some others, are simply of the brood of Molière. They may be said indeed to fall off from his style in this respect, that they show in their works no type of the time as he had showed the *marquis* and the *précieuses* and the *femmes savantes* of Louis' court. A distinct addition to Molière in this sense was not given until Lesage, in 1709, immortalised in *Turcaret* the type of the financier, lowborn, made important by his wealth, and courted for it by the hereditary aristocracy. The type has not yet become obsolete, and it has hardly been more successfully enshrined in literature than by the author of *Gil Blas*. Lesage had in him, no doubt, the stuff of much other portraiture of the same kind. But the actors of the Théâtre Français had become a power to which, as to other powers, the independent spirit of the novelist was not disposed to bend, and his dramatic talent was almost entirely diverted to the supply of trifles of the Vaudeville kind for the Théâtre de la Foire. His contemporary Destouches was less stiff-necked or more fortunate. He devoted himself almost entirely to the legitimate drama, and some of his work (*Le Glorieux, Le Philosophe Marié*, etc.) is of very high excellence. Another contemporary of Lesage, Piron, the wittiest epigrammatist of France, worked, like Lesage, chiefly for the irregular boards. But he produced one comedy in verse, *La Métromanie*, which became immediately a stock play, while many other authors who do not require separate mention followed in the general track.

The name of most importance, however, next in chronological order to Lesage is that of Marivaux. In the general style of Marivaux' plays there is, as has been already mentioned, no great difference from those ordinarily written in his time for the Théâtre Français, by which and by the Comédie Italienne he was indifferently employed. His chief idiosyncrasy lies in his style, which, though not entirely novel (for it had been anticipated to some extent by his friend and patron Fontenelle), struck his contemporaries sufficiently to receive a distinct title—that of *Marivaudage*. The peculiarities of *Marivaudage*, though in our own days they have shown themselves strongly in English literature itself, are not very easy to describe shortly in words. They may perhaps best be indicated by saying that the characters analyse their own thoughts and sentiments interminably, and express both in language which, though in Marivaux himself it is not devoid of charm, cannot escape the charge of affectation. Marivaux' plays are not ill-constructed, but the action is mainly subordinated to the display of this peculiar loquacity. He had some influence on his contemporaries, but on the whole not so much as might have been expected, till his peculiarities, reproduced to some extent by Richardson and Sterne, came back upon France by dint of the popularity which these two English novelists gained in that country during and after the third quarter of the century.

The successors of Marivaux, who, though not much influenced by him, were influenced not a little by the movement initiated by La Chaussée and Diderot (to be presently spoken of), were numerous, but their work hardly deserves individual mention except in the case of Sedaine, a writer of very considerable native talent, whose *Philosophe sans le Savoir* is one of the best French comedies which do not quite attain to the first class.

The most important name, historically speaking, of the eighteenth century in the list of comic writers, though by no means the most important from a purely literary point of view, is that of Beaumarchais. There is nothing in the general scheme of the *Barbier de Séville* and the *Mariage de Figaro* (which, though he wrote much else, are Beaumarchais' titles to fame) to distinguish them from other plays of their time and kind, nor is there much in their construction—eminently artistic from the playwright's point of view though it is—or even in their sparkling dialogue, which entitles them to this position of premiership. Beaumarchais' claim lies in the fact that for the first time since the reign of Louis XII he made the theatre a political engine. The whole drift of his two great plays is to satirise the privileged classes, not as Molière had done for foibles unconnected with their privileges or at most touching their social position, but from the political and rights-of-man point of view. Beaumarchais, a man not exactly of genius, but of extraordinary wit and talent, made the most of this application ; but it may be doubted whether the political comedy is not a degenerate form. In the other writers of the last quarter of the eighteenth century and the first quarter of the nineteenth absolutely no advance is made, indeed they may be said to relapse into conventional imitation of Molière. Collin d'Harléville, Andrieux, even Lemercier, obviously do not go directly to contemporary life or to the general notions of human weaknesses obtainable from observation of contemporary life for their subjects. They rely on their predecessors for types, and in their hands, as is inevitable, the types become a little blunter, a little less typical. There is still plenty of wit, but it is too much employed to broider a ready prepared canvas.

During the whole of the period thus summarised the drama of Molière was, as has been said, the model more or less of the playwright who aspired to regular comedy. But about the middle of the eighteenth century an attempt was made, chiefly by a dramatist of respectable talent, La Chaussée, and by a critic of great genius, Diderot, to strike out a new dramatic line in what was variously called *comédie larmoyante, tragédie bourgeoise,* and *drame.* This tended to the substitution of something still closer to nature, or to what the writers considered nature, than the subjects of the Molièresque drama. It is undeniable that in this drama, even of the most natural kind, a certain violence is still done to nature, so that pure comedy always becomes artificial comedy. When the rustic hero of *Sandford and Merton* was taken to see the *Marriage of Figaro,* and was asked his opinion of the piece, he replied with bluntness that it seemed to him that the people did nothing but lie, and cheat, and deceive, and that he could only suppose that if any lady or gentleman in real life had such a set of servants they would turn them off immediately. There is much truth in this as regards the Molièresque comedies of the decadence, when as usual the character of the play had become stereotyped. There is some truth in it even in regard to Molière's own comedies, where the fact that there are other passions in man than that of laughter is occasionally forgotten. La Chaussée and Diderot tried to make a kind of comedy of 'sensibility' as it was then termed, of the moral and domestic affections as we should say now. They did not succeed very well, but they at least indicated a blot in the Molièresque style when it is not at its very highest. Every literary class in all countries, and in France most of all, tends to become conventionalised, and it is only by continual reminders of the fact that it can be revivified. As a matter of fact the later comedy of the eighteenth century, though often amusing, is not very much less conventional than its tragedy. But fortunately for it the convention was based on types and models which, unlike those of tragedy, had originally abundant touches of nature.

Although no comedies of extraordinary merit had been produced for some half-century before the Preface of M. Victor Hugo's *Cromwell* definitely gave the programme of the romantic movement, the foregoing pages will have made it evident that no such outward change was likely or was required in comedy as in tragedy. Whatever disability may have weighed on the comic dramatist of 1825, weighed on him, not because of any hard and fast rules to which he was formally bound, but simply because he did not choose to avail himself of the liberty to which he was formally entitled, and to hold the mirror up to nature. Moreover, the strong romantic tendency (in the proper sense) of the time, that is to say, the desire to illustrate great passions and strong situations, was not favourable to comedy. The earliest effort of the great literary movement of 1830 directed itself, as far as the theatre was concerned, into tragedy or else *drame*, that is to say, in the older phrase, tragi-comedy. By degrees, however, a new and remarkable development of the comic theatre, showing the most distinct traces of the naturalism which was at the root of the romantic revolt, made itself apparent. The fault of the eighteenth-century comedy, and of all French comedy speaking generally, from Regnard to Andrieux, was its failure except in a few cases to mark sharply the changes of manners and of life. The heroes and heroines of the end of the eighteenth century are somehow or other identical in general characteristics with the heroes and heroines of the end of the seventeenth : in other words, what was nature in the earlier becomes convention in the later. The men of 1830 quickly changed this. For conventional personages and manners, often amusingly enough handled, but very difficult to put into definite chronological circumstances, they once more substituted copies from the life. It so happened that only one of the greatest men of the original 'generation of 1830' produced properly comic work of great merit, but this was work of very great merit indeed. The comedies, and still more the *Proverbes*, of Alfred de Musset are in some respects the most original things of their kind since the time of Molière. They restored to comedy the poetical element which had long been lacking to it in French, which had indeed in that language never been prominent in it. In the *Proverbes* especially—short pieces in which some proverbial maxim is exemplified and worked out by a dramatic application—a wonderful liveliness of touch and delicacy of dramatic fancy is apparent. Those who judge all things from the technical point of view of the playwright or the actor sometimes affect to disparage these dainty plays in miniature, just as other persons of the same stamp sometimes tell us in England that Shakespeare did not really write good plays, but only good literature. But the public, though rather slowly, has done Musset justice, and among properly quali-fied literary critics his position could never have been matter of doubt. His peculiar style of writing is as much a genuine kind of true comedy as Molière's own. But it must be noted that one of the innovations of 1830 was to break down (following in this respect and improving upon the already mentioned upholders of *comédie larmoyante*) the old rigid canon that a comedy must have a good ending and a tragedy a bad one, so that not a few pieces after 1833 would have been refused the title of comedy before that date. This more especially applies to Musset, who rarely writes without a touch of tragedy. Thus, for instance, the exquisite *On ne badine pas avec l'amour*, comic in motive almost throughout, ends with a sharp and sudden, though perfectly natural, tragic turn. Perhaps the most remarkable thing about Musset as a dramatist (and in this he has pretty generally been followed, at least in intention, by his successors) is, that his wit, brilliant as it is, constantly and after a fashion more usual with English humour than with French wit, passes thus rapidly and naturally into tears. The modern comedy, except of the purely farcical sort, is therefore a more mixed kind than the older, and is perhaps a little inferior to it in artistic

D

proportion and completeness. But what it loses in these respects it undoubtedly gains in verisimilitude and in appealing not merely to the faculty of laughter, but to the nobler sympathies of man.

The dramatists of the last half-century are so numerous, and the lines on which they have worked have been so wide and diverse, that an account of them in a few lines is not easy to give. Indeed, as far as form is concerned, it is not so much difficult as impossible, for during the whole period dramatists, and comic dramatists especially, have been practically free to follow or to invent for themselves any patterns they chose. There have resulted perhaps few plays that posterity will read, as posterity has read Molière, or even as it has read Marivaux, but many which have had singular acting success, and not a few which have had singular acting merit. In the lightest kind of comedy the most prominent writers of the century have been Eugène Scribe, and following him Eugène Labiche. The first, with a hardly surpassable faculty of divining and satisfying the taste of his day, came decidedly short of the perfection of style which lasting work demands, and this was all the more remarkable as he not unfrequently essayed comedy of a somewhat dignified kind. M. Labiche, aiming as a rule at the lightest of light comedy only, has succeeded in elaborating a style so admirably fitted to it that he has not undeservedly been elected to the Academy, and that his work, as far as it is possible to its kind, is not unlikely to go down to the future unforgotten. In this same lighter kind of comedy an immense volume of work has been produced, including some in a kind almost peculiar to the time, such as the musical burlesques of Offenbach, which, thanks to the excellent librettos composed for them by MM. Meilhac and Halévy, deserve some rank in literature as well as in the class of social documents. M. Gondinet is another writer of light comedy deserving mention, and still more M. Pailleron, the latter of whom in some slight pieces, such as *Le Chevalier Trumeau*, has succeeded in uniting the best characteristics of the eighteenth-century tale with those of the *Proverbe* after Musset's fashion. It should be noted as being far from unimportant that the connection between novel-writing and play-writing has in these latter days been very close, a successful novel being more often than not dramatised either by the author himself or by him in collaboration with a more practised dramatist.

There are three comic, or chiefly comic, dramatists who in more elaborate work rank far ahead of all others during the latter part of the period now under review, and these three exhibit to the fullest extent the peculiarity of the whole time, that is to say, the close copying of contemporary ideas and manners. They are Alexandre Dumas *fils*, Emile Augier, and Victorien Sardou. Alexandre Dumas—the son of the still greater novelist of that name, who was himself one of the most accomplished dramatists of the century, though hardly in comic matter—has particularly taken up half-political, half-ethical questions, and has worked them out doubtless with much talent, but in a spirit of determined moralising and purpose (enforced in the printed plays by very characteristic prefaces) which occasionally interferes with their dramatic, and still more with their literary merit. M. Emile Augier, on the whole the foremost dramatist of the time, has escaped this danger, though he also reflects the moral and social characteristics of his time very powerfully. But the literary spirit of the best kind is strong in M. Augier, and in such plays as *L'Aventurière, Le fils de Giboyer,* and *Le Gendre de M. Poirier* (which he wrote in collaboration with the novelist Sandeau, and which is based on a prose fiction of the latter's) he succeeds in doing what is most difficult, giving exact portraiture of fleeting and ephemeral peculiarities without so much descent into detail as is likely to make the portraits obsolete when the originals are forgotten. As a rule this is the weak point of the drama of these days, and M. Augier himself cannot be said to be wholly free from the weakness. The third dramatist mentioned, M. Sardou, is the most unequal and also the most unoriginal of the three. But his *Famille Benoiton* is likely to remain a *locus classicus* for the representation of the worse side, socially speaking, of the second Empire, and his *Rabagas* gives a sketch of the successful demagogue which is, as few things of our time are, sufficiently imbued with perennial and not merely fleeting colours to last.

These three writers display in themselves pretty fully the general characteristics of the comic drama in France to-day, though for a complete view they require to be supplemented by M. Labiche for light work of the older and more *bourgeois* kind, M. Pailleron for that of the latest 'elegant' society, and M. Halévy for burlesque. There are very many other dramatists who, if the purpose here were to give a dictionary of the French drama, would have to be mentioned, but who, the purpose being what it is, scarcely need mention. It should, however, be observed that M. Feuillet, the now veteran novelist, is also an exceedingly skilful adapter of his own novels. It is necessary to take this close connection between novel and drama together with the constantly increasing realism of the novel. It may be open to doubt whether as at some times the conventionalities of literary standards have led the novelist and still more the dramatist too much away from actual life, so at the present time the habit of copying what is or is thought to be actual has not in the drama as elsewhere led to a forgetfulness that photography is not art, that art is not a mere reproduction of nature, and that if it attempts to be this it loses much of the interest and more of the beauty which should belong to it. But as the theatre at its best has always clung very closely to the facts of life, and as comedy in particular must be in the main a reproduction of those facts, the mischief is perhaps less here than it is in some other departments of literature. Though it has not a few grave drawbacks, the present value of French comedy is positively considerable, and relatively still more so; and if it is not higher, this must be set down to the accidental fact that no man of the highest genius has lately made it his province.

The especial object and use of such a brief summary of the history of French comedy as this is not merely to give the student a bird's-eye view of the principal forms and names which have illustrated its progress. It is rather that he may understand the remarkable and unique unity which prevails throughout it. There is no doubt that of modern

nations France is the special home of comedy. Other
countries have either produced occasional masterpieces due
to imitation of Molière, such as the works of Congreve and
his contemporaries, or artificial pieces like the Italian comedy
of the eighteenth century, and the English humour comedy
of the early seventeenth, or else romantic and poetical
drama like that of Shakespeare and Calderon, the main
merits of which are not comic but romantic and poetical. But
in France the comic writer from the thirteenth century
downwards has never been very far from pure comedy, which
may be defined as the dramatic representation of the
ludicrous side of actual life. At one time this definition has
been more closely adhered to and more intelligently inter-
preted than at another: one period has produced workmen
of greater talent or greater genius than another. But it has
never been wholly lost sight of; and thus, the conditions
of the form being natural, not artificial, it has preserved
throughout a striking likeness to itself—a likeness totally
wanting in the case of tragedy, which is at the best a
somewhat artificial thing, and which in the hands of French
dramatists has always been artificial in a high degree. The
comedy has of course been better or worse according to
circumstances. When dramatists tried to imitate the highly
conventional drama of Terence, or to transfer to France the
complicated intrigues of Spain; or when they contented
themselves with simply ringing the changes on the situations of Molière or other great writers, the drama languished.
When they shook off these trammels and went back to the
life of their own day or to the general and perennial characteristics of humanity, it flourished. But it is very curious and
instructive to compare the immense number of different
names which comic writing has borne and still bears in
France with the real similarity which runs through all the
kinds to which they correspond. Moreover, with the exception of the prose fiction of the last half-century, it would
probably be impossible to mention any branch of literature
the productions of which are relatively, and in proportion to
the excellence attainable, so uniformly good as the works of
French comic writers. The suitableness of the national

language to comic dialogue, of the national manners to comic action, of the national intellect to the comprehension and arrangement of the comic plot, have all helped to produce this result. The difficulty with which French adapts itself to the expression of the highest poetry is not felt in comedy. The main faults of the French character, its want of reverence, of reticence, of depth of feeling, are not felt here. Indeed they are positive stimulants to the production and the enjoyment of comedy. Moreover, the propensity for moralising, which oddly enough accompanies these defects, is useful in comic writing, and sometimes, as in the case of Molière, it produces the very best and highest kind of comic work—the work which in satirising preaches but without dulness, and in preaching satirises but without scurrility. Therefore it is that these forces remaining the same and being for the most part left to their natural working the work produced is remarkably alike. When in the first French comedy Adam de la Halle draws the enchantment and the disenchantment of husband and wife, or the petty jealousies of neighbours, he not only takes very much the same subjects as M. Pailleron and M. Sardou at the present day; but, with due allowance made, he treats them in by no means a very different manner. There is the progress of manners, refinement, and language, the change of society, the experience of six centuries in play-writing to be taken account of, but there is very little else: certainly there is infinitely less than is the case in other departments of literature.

III. The Comic Stage in the Age of Molière.

WHEN Molière arrived in Paris in 1658 he found three troupes in possession of the town. First came the troupe of the Hôtel de Bourgogne, the successors of the old religious *Confrères de la Passion.* This company's house was in the angle between the Rue Mauconseil and the Rue Française. In 1868 all that remained of the house was the café in No. 7, Rue Française. Louis Treize had granted to the company the title of *Troupe Royale*, of which they were not a little vain. They possessed, or exercised, the right of impressing recruits from the other French company, that of the Marais, which had been established nearly fifty years before the arrival of Molière. The company of the Marais played at various times in various theatres, but, in 1635, settled down in a tennis-court in the Rue Vieille du Temple. It is melancholy to note how, as France became modern France, the tennis-courts ceased to be used for their natural purpose. The love of manly sports declined long before the Revolution gave, practically, the deathblow to tennis. The Marais theatre was closed after the death of Molière, in 1673, and some of the players joined *les Grands Comédiens*, of the Hôtel de Bourgogne, some entered the troupe of Molière's widow. The Italian company, with which Molière shared a theatre (playing on alternate days), did not act regular dramas. They knew the outline of the piece they were to perform, and the actors took their parts as in a modern 'charade.' Of the three companies the Hôtel de Bourgogne naturally had the most popular authors (as Corneille) at its command, but Corneille was first produced at the Marais.

The company of Molière first obtained a half-share, with the Italians, in the Hôtel du Petit Bourbon. This house had belonged to the Constable de Bourbon, and was confiscated and daubed all over with yellow paint (the livery of disgrace), after his treachery under Francis I. The hall stood between the old Louvre and St. Germain l'Auxerrois, on the right of the Louvre as it is at present. The *grande salle* of the Hôtel was the room in which Molière's company acted. In 1660 the building was demolished, and the company moved into the *salle* of the Palais Royal, then in terrible disrepair. This was, however, the only place of entertainment in Paris which had been built for theatrical purposes. Molière was his own author in chief. When he played another man's piece he usually gave him two actors' shares of the receipts. To Corneille in old age he gave 2000 livres for *Attila*; to Boyer, for *Tonnaxare* (which was damned) he gave 550 livres in a purse embroidered with gold.

What were the gains of an actor in Molière's troupe? La Grange tells us that, in fourteen years' work, he got 51,670 livres. Part of this came from his share of receipts when the company acted in public, part from the presents made to the actors when they paid a visit to some great man's house, and played for the amusement of his guests. In ordinary years, a member of Molière's company received 3000 livres, or more. Molière, as an author, with his author's double share (till he resigned it), and the profits from his plays when printed, made a considerable fortune. As to state aid, or rather Royal aid, the Hôtel de Bourgogne received, or was owed, 12000 livres annually. The Italian company received 15000 livres, that of Molière (after 1665) 6000 livres, afterwards raised to 7000. The price for places in the theatre varied with the accommodation. In the pit people paid 15 sous for standing room (sometimes doubled on 'first nights'), and half a louis d'or for a chair on the stage, among the actors, though 'that spoils all,' as Tallemant says. Chappuzeau, on the other hand, thought the presence of the rich on the stage a great ornament! A very full house was reckoned at about 2000 livres. *Tartuffe* drew a house of 2045 livres, when revived after its suppression. On the first night of the *Malade Imaginaire* there were 1992 livres in the house.

Not much attention was paid to stage effect and scenery. When Thomiris called *À moi, soldats!* the advance of the Scythian levies was indicated by a painting of an army, which was drawn over an impracticable bridge. There were no foot-lights, only chandeliers. The actors could only enter on the scene from the bottom of the stage. More money and more care was expended on the great spectacular pieces *à machines.* As to archaeological accuracy, no one ever dreamed of attaining it. As late as 1811, a modern inkstand with quill pens was placed on the table of Agamemnon! And this was after Wolf's celebrated *Prolegomena*, in which it may be said to be demonstrated that the Homeric age did not use quill pens.

If the scenery was scanty, the costumes were most magnificent in the gorgeous taste of the day. Ribbons, Venice lace, gold embroidery, and feathers were not spared. Varied refreshments were sold in the house. Did the audience smoke? They certainly threw clay pipes at unpopular players. Organized hooting with *sifflets* is said to have come in when Fontenelle's *Aspar* was damned in 1680. Hissing, however, was much older, also pelting with apples, usually roasted. Taking one consideration with another, as he was liable to be hooted, pelted, stabbed by angry *mousquetaires,* and refused Christian burial, an actor's life was not wholly a happy one, even when Molière ruled the town and the court of France.

IV. INTRODUCTION TO LES PRÉCIEUSES RIDICULES.

ON November 18, 1659, the large playbills outside the Théâtre du Petit Bourbon announced *Cinna* and *Les Précieuses Ridicules.* It was the 'first night' of the new comedy, and the theatre, as we gather from the *Registre* of La Grange, was not well filled. Yet people interested in the stage might have known (the name of the comedy alone should have told them) that there was to be an attack on the *Précieuses.* By this time the name *Précieuses* was almost as well known to satire as that of 'Aesthetes' was a year or two ago in England. The Abbé de Pure, as early as 1656, had composed a novel styled *La Précieuse, ou le Mystère de la Ruelle,* and in the same year the Italian players in Paris had a 'canvas' taken from the story of De Pure. The Italians did not act regular plays, but each understood the general drift of the piece, and supplied most of his own part by his own cleverness, as in a modern acted charade. Molière was, of course, accused of stealing from this drama, and, in the *Véritables Précieuses,* by Somaize, one of the characters tries to prove that there is a close resemblance between the piece of Molière and that played by the Italians. Such charges are always brought against the author of every successful new comedy. The topic is only worth mentioning as a proof (if proof were needed) that before Molière produced his piece the word *précieuse* indicated a well-known butt, the learned and affected lady of letters. Chapelain and Bachaumont had found provincial *Précieuses* at Montpellier, before Molière produced his piece in Paris. These *Précieuses* of Montpellier

> croyaient Monsieur de Scuderis
> Un homme de fort bonne mine,
> Sa sœur une beauté divine,

and they said that Ménage

> Avait l'air et l'esprit galant.

In short, the public of Paris recognised in the *Précieuses* ladies who aimed at a reputation for taste, were very choice in their phrases, and admired the works of the Scudéry and of the learned fribble Ménage. De Pure had already said (and his words oddly fit our modern representatives of the *Précieuses*), 'La Précieuse se forme dans la Ruelle *par la culture.*'

The original *Précieuses*, who set the literary and social fashions, were the society of the Hôtel Rambouillet. La Rochefoucauld, Chapelain (that epic failure), Cotin (later travestied as Trissotin in *Les Femmes Savantes*), Segrais, Bussy Rabutin (who at least was not a prig), Ménage, Vaugelas, Benserade, wits, fops, grammarians, scholars, were all frequenters of the Hôtel Rambouillet. The society had thus far more than the brilliance, if it was not without the defects, of most 'circles' and 'cliques.' Like all such côteries, it was corrupted by narrow pedantry within, and hated by jealous and 'robustious' dulness without. There could scarcely be better game for satire. Madame de Rambouillet, 'the incomparable Arthénice,' had been the head of the society. She had attempted to reform the extraordinary rudeness of manners which amazes us in the *Historiettes* of Tallemant.

Her attempt had not been fruitless, but the refinement of her friends and associates had merged itself in a kind of Euphuism of language and affectation of manners. Love had been deprived, perhaps, of its too rough-and-ready character, but the new substitute of long courtships, *billets galants, petits-soins,* and all the voyage down *le fleuve de Tendre,* was scarcely an improvement.

Between 1648 and 1655, after the marriage of the fair Julie, the death of Voiture, and the death of the old Marquis de Rambouillet, the Hôtel ceased to be the general resort of men of letters who were in society, and of society which concerned itself with letters. *Ruelles* and alcoves (*boudoirs* and *salons* of the time) began to multiply, and, with numbers, to lose distinction. Visitors were generally received in the bed-room, a custom that appears far from refined to modern taste. The bed-chamber was divided into two parts, a balustrade separating the half which contained the bed from the rest of the room. Alcoves too were invented, small spaces opening off a larger chamber, and ladies received their friends either in the alcove or the *ruelle,* the open space in the bedroom. Arm-chairs (*fauteuils*) were offered to the more distinguished guests, and many quarrels arose among ladies as to who had the best right to a *fauteuil.* Sometimes the men lay at the feet of the ladies. The conversation was (as we learn from the *Précieuses Ridicules*) like the 'Literary Gossip' in a weekly review. Who was engaged on a poem, who on a play, who was correcting his proof-sheets, who was the author of the last anonymous tale, who contributed to this or that *recueil* of select pieces?—such matters interested women who, as Keats says, 'would have liked to marry a novel, and be given away by a poem.'

> *A peu près voicy les nouvelles*
> *Qu'on débite dans les ruelles.*

Letters from absent friends were read aloud, and, being full of gossip, supplied the place of the society journals, such as the *Mercure Galant,* started not very long afterwards. In literature there was excessive concern about style. The *Précieuses* introduced many turns of expression which have become familiar. Such turns or words are *le mot me manque, un esprit à expédients, superfluité, châtier son style, dépenser une heure, il a de l'esprit, tour d'esprit, agir sans façon, faire des avances.* Less fortunate expressions and phrases (as absurd as our ancient Euphuism, or the Latinisms of the Limousin in Rabelais) are illustrated in Molière's play. It contains many examples of the affected style of talk which has arisen in a new shape, and been ridiculed anew, here in England. A servant, in place of giving a guest a chair, was told *voiturer les commodités de la conversation.* A mirror was *le conseiller des Grâces.* In fact, the love of periphrasis, a form of bad taste as old as the sagas, was in full force among the *Précieuses.* They patronised modish trifles of literature, enigmas, portraits, letters, and, for more solid reading, chose interminable romances of a faded and mannered chivalry, the works of Mlle. de Scudéry being the chief favourites.

A society of this kind, with its pet *abbés* ('alcovistes' they were called, and *introducteurs des ruelles*), seemed to call out for satire. The *Précieuses* had passed the point at which their great exemplar, Madame de Rambouillet, had been of real service to society and literature. They had become so well known that even the public at large had heard of them, and was able to understand jests directed at their failings. Yet the theatre was not crowded on the first night, nor does it seem certain, though Ménage vouches for it, that 'tout le cabinet de l'hôtel de Rambouillet' was present, including Chapelain and Madame de Grignan. According to Ménage he himself observed to Chapelain, 'After this comedy we must burn what we had adored, and adore what we were wont to burn,' but the anecdote is suspected of being an afterthought. He, or his editor, says (*Menagiana*, 1729; i. 144) that Molière's own prose is full of *expressions précieuses;* this sounds a little rancorous; and, in the same place, Ménage tells a story all to his own advantage about *Tartuffe.* He had assured Lamoignon when the President stopped the play, that the moral of *Tartuffe* 'was excellent.' It is Ménage who calls Molière *grand et habile picoreur,* a snapper-up of unconsidered literary trifles. Molière had even stolen an idea of Ménage's own (ii. 197), though Ménage has the grace to admit that the notion was public property. He preferred Perrault's poem on the art of painting to that of Molière. Lastly, Ménage clearly believed himself to have been the model for the Vadius of *Les Femmes Savantes*. Thus, on the whole, whatever he says about himself and Molière must be taken with caution, and we need not believe that the society of the Hôtel Rambouillet went to the first night of the *Précieuses*, merely on the evidence of Ménage. From that night, he insists, people deserted their old *galimatias*, and forced style. Furetière, however, six years later found *précieuses* still thriving among the *bourgeoises* of Paris.

Another anecdote about the first night of the *Précieuses* is too well known to be omitted. An old man is said to have stood up and cried, 'Courage, Molière, voilà enfin de la bonne comédie.'

Successful or not on its first night, the piece was stopped, apparently by some intrigue. The king was in the Pyrenees, and his unfailing protection was wanting to Molière. Played first on November 18, the *Précieuses* was laid aside till December 2, and, apparently, had to be somewhat altered before its second appearance. This is inferred from the *Récit*, or account of the performance, by Mlle. de Jardins, who appears to have been present at the first representation. This lady gives the following lively account of the entrance of Mascarille :—'Imagine, Madame, his mighty wig, that swept the floor whenever he made a bow, and the little hat, so small you might easily see the Marquis carried it more in his hand than on his head. His bands were as large as a pretty big peignoir, and his *canons* might have served children to play hide and seek in. A bunch of tassels stuck out of his pocket, as big as a cornucopia, and his shoes were so covered with ribbons that you could not tell whether the leather was English calf or morocco. All I know is that they were half a foot high, and that I was much put to it to conceive how such slim high heels could bear the weight of the Marquis, his ribbons, his *canons*, and his powder.' The frontispiece prefixed to this play, a reduced copy of the frontispiece of 1682, shows Mascarille in all his glory.

In spite of the prohibition, which was removed in about a fortnight, the *Précieuses*, once seen, was extremely successful. Thomas Corneille grudgingly admits that crowds flocked to the play, 'which proves,' he added, 'that *Messieurs de Bourbon* can only act in trifles.' Often the company performed the *Précieuses, en visite* at the houses of the great. When the king returned from the Pyrenees, *L'Étourdi* and *Les Précieuses* were the first pieces Molière played before him. On October 26 the piece was acted at the house of Mazarin, 'qui étoit malade en sa chaise.' The young king looked on as he stood beside the cardinal's chair; the rising sun behind the red sunset of the priestly ruler,—

L'écarlate linceul du pâle Mazarin.

Though played fifty-three times in two years, the *Précieuses* was only thrice acted afterwards during the lifetime of Molière. It went out of fashion, for the moment, when the *Précieuses* had been laughed down. But 'preciousness' is always reviving, in the age of *Le Monde où l'on s'ennuie*, as in that of Molière, and the satire is always in season.

The actors in the original cast were La Grange, Molière's friend and biographer ; Du Croisy ; Jodelet (who died March 26, 1660) ; Molière himself, and, probably, Mlle. de Brie as Madelon, and Madeleine Béjart as Marotte. But this is more or less guesswork. At present M. Coquelin takes the part of Mascarille, and the younger Coquelin is Jodelet. Madame Dinah Félix is usually Cathos.

LES
PRÉCIEUSES RIDICULES.

COMÉDIE
EN UN ACTE ET EN PROSE

PAR

MOLIÈRE

1659

PERSONNAGES.

LA GRANGE (1), } amants rebutés.
DU CROISY (2),

GORGIBUS (3), bon bourgeois.

MAGDELON, fille de Gorgibus (4), } Précieuses ridicules.
CATHOS, nièce de Gorgibus (5),

MAROTTE, servante des Précieuses ridicules (6).

ALMANZOR, laquais des Précieuses ridicules (7).

LE MARQUIS DE MASCARILLE, valet de La Grange (8).

LE VICOMTE DE JODELET, valet de Du Croisy (9).

Deux Porteurs de Chaise.

Voisines.

Violons.

La scène est à Paris, dans la maison de Gorgibus.

———————

Acteurs de la troupe de Molière :

(1) La Grange.   (5) Mademoiselle du Parc.
(2) Du Croisy.   (6) Madeleine Béjart.
(3) L'Espy.   (7) De Brie.
(4) Mademoiselle de Brie. (8) Molière.
              (9) Brécourt.

PRÉFACE DE L'AUTEUR.

C'EST une chose étrange qu'on imprime les gens malgré eux. Je ne vois rien de si injuste, et je pardonnerois toute autre violence plutôt que celle-là.

Ce n'est pas que je veuille faire ici l'auteur modeste, et mépriser par honneur ma comédie. J'offenserois mal à pro- 5 pos tout Paris, si je l'accusois d'avoir pu applaudir à une sottise. Comme le public est le juge absolu de ces sortes d'ouvrages, il y auroit de l'impertinence à moi de le démentir ; et quand j'aurois eu la plus mauvaise opinion du monde de mes *Précieuses ridicules* avant leur représentation, je dois 10 croire maintenant qu'elles valent quelque chose, puisque tant de gens ensemble en ont dit du bien. Mais comme une grande partie des grâces qu'on y a trouvées dépendent de l'action et du ton de voix, il m'importoit qu'on ne les dépouillât pas de ces ornements ; et je trouvois que le succès qu'elles 15 avoient eu dans la représentation étoit assez beau, pour en demeurer là. J'avois résolu, dis-je, de ne les faire voir qu'à la chandelle, pour ne point donner lieu à quelqu'un de dire le proverbe ; et je ne voulois pas qu'elles sautassent du théâtre de Bourbon dans la galerie du Palais. Cependant je n'ai pu 20 l'éviter, et je suis tombé dans la disgrâce de voir une copie dérobée de ma pièce entre les mains des libraires accompagnée d'un privilége obtenu par surprise. J'ai eu beau crier : 'O temps, ô mœurs !' on m'a fait voir une nécessité pour moi d'être imprimé, ou d'avoir un procès ; et le dernier 25 mal est encore pire que le premier. Il faut donc se laisser aller à la destinée, et consentir à une chose qu'on ne laisseroit pas de faire sans moi.

Mon Dieu ! l'étrange embarras qu'un livre à mettre au jour, et qu'un auteur est neuf la première fois qu'on l'imprime ! 30 Encore si l'on m'avoit donné du temps, j'aurois pu mieux

songer à moi, et j'aurois pris toutes les précautions que Messieurs les auteurs, à présent mes confrères, ont coutume de prendre en semblables occasions. Outre quelque grand seigneur que j'aurois été prendre malgré lui pour protecteur de
5 mon ouvrage, et dont j'aurois tenté la libéralité par une épître dédicatoire bien fleurie, j'aurois tâché de faire une belle et docte préface ; et je ne manque point de livres qui m'auroient fourni tout ce qu'on peut dire de savant sur la tragédie et la comédie, l'étymologie de toutes deux, leur origine, leur défi-
10 nition et le reste. J'aurois parlé aussi à mes amis, qui pour la recommandation de ma pièce ne m'auroient pas refusé ou des vers françois, ou des vers latins. J'en ai même qui m'auroient loué en grec ; et l'on n'ignore pas qu'une louange en grec est d'une merveilleuse efficace à la tête d'un livre.
15 Mais on me met au jour sans me donner le loisir de me reconnoître ; et je ne puis même obtenir la liberté de dire deux mots pour justifier mes intentions sur le sujet de cette comédie. J'aurois voulu faire voir qu'elle se tient partout dans les bornes de la satire honnête et permise ; que les plus excel-
20 lentes choses sont sujettes à être copiées par de mauvais singes, qui méritent d'être bernés ; que ces vicieuses imitations de ce qu'il y a de plus parfait ont été de tout temps la matière de la comédie ; et que, par la même raison que les véritables savants et les vrais braves ne se sont point encore
25 avisés de s'offenser du Docteur de la comédie et du Capitan, non plus que les juges, les princes et les rois de voir Trivelin, ou quelque autre sur le théâtre, faire ridiculement le juge, le prince ou le roi, aussi les véritables précieuses auroient tort de se piquer lorsqu'on joue les ridicules qui les imitent mal.
30 Mais enfin, comme j'ai dit, on ne me laisse pas le temps de respirer, et M. de Luynes veut m'aller relier de ce pas : à la bonne heure, puisque Dieu l'a voulu.

LES
PRÉCIEUSES RIDICULES.

SCÈNE PREMIÈRE.

LA GRANGE, DU CROISY.

Du Croisy. Seigneur la Grange.

La Grange. Quoi ?

Du Croisy. · Regardez-moi un peu sans rire.

La Grange. Eh bien ?

Du Croisy. Que dites-vous de notre visite ! en êtes-vous 5
fort satisfait ?

La Grange. A votre avis, avons-nous sujet de l'être tous
deux ?

Du Croisy. Pas tout à fait, à dire vrai.

La Grange. Pour moi, je vous avoue que j'en suis tout 10
scandalisé. A-t-on jamais vu, dites-moi, deux pecques pro-
vinciales faire plus les renchéries que celles-là, et deux
hommes traités avec plus de mépris que nous ? A peine ont-
elles pu se résoudre à nous faire donner des siéges. Je n'ai
jamais vu tant parler à l'oreille qu'elles ont fait entre elles, 15
tant bâiller, tant se frotter les yeux, et demander tant de fois :
'Quelle heure est-il ?' Ont-elles répondu que, oui et non, à
tout ce que nous avons pu leur dire ? Et ne m'avouerez-
vous pas enfin que, quand nous aurions été les dernières
personnes du monde, on ne pouvoit nous faire pis qu'elles 20
ont fait ?

Du Croisy. Il me semble que vous prenez la chose fort à
cœur.

La Grange. Sans doute je l'y prends, et de telle façon que je veux me venger de cette impertinence. Je connois ce qui nous a fait mépriser. L'air précieux n'a pas seulement infecté Paris, il s'est aussi répandu dans les provinces, et
5 nos donzelles ridicules en ont humé leur bonne part. En un mot, c'est un ambigu de précieuse et de coquette que leur personne. Je vois ce qu'il faut être pour en être bien reçu ; et si vous m'en croyez, nous leur jouerons tous deux une pièce qui leur fera voir leur sottise, et pourra leur apprendre à con-
10 noître un peu mieux leur monde.

Du Croisy. Et comment encore ?

La Grange. J'ai un certain valet, nommé Mascarille, qui passe, au sentiment de beaucoup de gens, pour une manière de bel esprit ; car il n'y a rien à meilleur marché que le bel
15 esprit maintenant. C'est un extravagant, qui s'est mis dans la tête de vouloir faire l'homme de condition. Il se pique ordinairement de galanterie et de vers, et dédaigne les autres valets, jusqu'à les appeler brutaux.

Du Croisy. Eh bien, qu'en prétendez-vous faire ?

20 *La Grange.* Ce que j'en prétends faire ? Il faut... Mais sortons d'ici auparavant.

SCÈNE II.

Gorgibus, Du Croisy, La Grange.

Gorgibus. Eh bien, vous avez vu ma nièce et ma fille, les affaires iront-elles bien ? Quel est le résultat de cette visite ?

25 *La Grange.* C'est une chose que vous pourrez mieux apprendre d'elles que de nous. Tout ce que nous pouvons vous dire, c'est que nous vous rendons grâce de la faveur que vous nous avez faite, et demeurons vos très-humbles serviteurs.

Gorgibus. Ouais, il semble qu'ils sortent mal satisfaits
30 d'ici. D'où pourroit venir leur mécontentement ? Il faut savoir un peu ce que c'est. Holà !

SCÈNE III.

MAROTTE, GORGIBUS.

Marotte. Que désirez-vous, Monsieur ?

Gorgibus. Où sont vos maîtresses ?

Marotte. Dans leur cabinet.

Gorgibus. Que font-elles ?

Marotte. De la pommade pour les lèvres. 5

Gorgibus. C'est trop pommadé : dites-leur qu'elles descendent. Ces pendardes-là, avec leur pommade, ont, je pense, envie de me ruiner. Je ne vois partout que blancs d'œufs, lait virginal, et mille autres brimborions que je ne connois point. Elles ont usé, depuis que nous sommes ici, 10 le lard d'une douzaine de cochons, pour le moins, et quatre valets vivroient tous les jours des pieds de mouton qu'elles emploient.

SCÈNE IV.

MAGDELON, CATHOS, GORGIBUS.

Gorgibus. Il est bien nécessaire vraiment de faire tant de dépense pour vous graisser le museau. Dites-moi un peu 15 ce que vous avez fait à ces messieurs, que je les vois sortir avec tant de froideur ? Vous avois-je pas commandé de les recevoir comme des personnes que je voulois vous donner pour maris ?

Magdelon. Et quelle estime, mon père, voulez-vous que 20 nous fassions du procédé irrégulier de ces gens-là ?

Cathos. Le moyen, mon oncle, qu'une fille un peu raisonnable se pût accommoder de leur personne ?

Gorgibus. Et qu'y trouvez-vous à redire ?

Magdelon. La belle galanterie que la leur ! Quoi ? débu- 25 ter d'abord par le mariage !

Gorgibus. Et par où veux-tu donc qu'ils débutent? par le concubinage? N'est-ce pas un procédé dont vous avez sujet de vous louer toutes deux aussi bien que moi? Est-il rien de plus obligeant que cela? Et ce lien sacré où ils aspirent
5 n'est-il pas un témoignage de l'honnêteté de leurs intentions?

Magdelon. Ah! mon père, ce que vous dites là est du dernier bourgeois. Cela me fait honte de vous ouïr parler de la sorte, et vous devriez un peu vous faire apprendre le bel air
10 des choses.

Gorgibus. Je n'ai que faire ni d'air ni de chanson. Je te dis que le mariage est une chose sainte et sacrée, et que c'est faire en honnêtes gens que de débuter par là.

Magdelon. Mon Dieu, que si tout le monde vous ressem-
15 bloit, un roman seroit bientôt fini! La belle chose que ce seroit si d'abord Cyrus épousoit Mandane, et qu'Aronce de plain-pied fût marié à Clélie!

Gorgibus. Que me vient conter celle-ci?

Magdelon. Mon père, voilà ma cousine, qui vous dira, aussi
20 bien que moi, que le mariage ne doit jamais arriver qu'après les autres aventures. Il faut qu'un amant, pour être agréable, sache débiter les beaux sentiments, pousser le doux, le tendre et le passionné, et que sa recherche soit dans les formes. Premièrement, il doit voir au temple, ou à la promenade, ou
25 dans quelque cérémonie publique, la personne dont il devient amoureux; ou bien être conduit fatalement chez elle par un parent ou un ami, et sortir de là tout rêveur et mélancolique. Il cache un temps sa passion à l'objet aimé, et cependant lui rend plusieurs visites, où l'on ne manque jamais de mettre
30 sur le tapis une question galante qui exerce les esprits de l'assemblée. Le jour de la déclaration arrive, qui se doit faire ordinairement dans une allée de quelque jardin, tandis que la compagnie s'est un peu éloignée : et cette déclaration est suivie d'un prompt courroux, qui paroît à notre rougeur, et
35 qui pour un temps bannit l'amant de notre présence. En-suite il trouve moyen de nous apaiser, de nous accoutumer

insensiblement au discours de sa passion, et de tirer de nous cet aveu qui fait tant de peine. Après cela viennent les aventures, les rivaux qui se jettent à la traverse d'une inclination établie, les persécutions des pères, les jalousies conçues sur de fausses apparences, les plaintes, les désespoirs, les enléve- 5 ments, et ce qui s'ensuit. Voilà comme les choses se traitent dans les belles manières, et ce sont des règles dont, en bonne galanterie, on ne sauroit se dispenser. Mais en venir de but en blanc à l'union conjugale, ne faire l'amour qu'en faisant le contrat du mariage, et prendre justement le roman 10 par la queue ! encore un coup mon père, il ne se peut rien de plus marchand que ce procédé, et j'ai mal au cœur de la seule vision que cela me fait.

Gorgibus. Quel diable de jargon entends-je ici ? Voici bien du haut style. 15

Cathos. En effet, mon oncle, ma cousine donne dans le vrai de la chose. Le moyen de bien recevoir des gens qui sont tout à fait incongrus en galanterie ? Je m'en vais gager qu'ils n'ont jamais vu la carte de Tendre, et que Billets-Doux, Petits-Soins, Billets-Galants et Jolis-Vers sont des terres in- 20 connues pour eux. Ne voyez-vous pas que toute leur personne marque cela, et qu'ils n'ont point cet air qui donne d'abord bonne opinion des gens ? Venir en visite amoureuse avec une jambe toute unie, un chapeau désarmé de plumes, une tête irrégulière en cheveux, et un habit qui souffre une 25 indigence de rubans ! mon Dieu, quels amants sont-ce là ! Quelle frugalité d'ajustement, et quelle sécheresse de conversation ! On n'y dure point, on n'y tient pas. J'ai remarqué encore que leurs rabats ne sont pas de la bonne faiseuse, et qu'il s'en faut plus d'un grand demipied que leurs hauts- 30 dechausses ne soient assez larges.

Gorgibus. Je pense qu'elles sont folles toutes deux, et je ne puis rien comprendre à ce baragouin. Cathos, et vous, Magdelon ...

Magdelon. Eh, de grâce, mon père, défaites-vous de ces 35 noms étranges, et nous appelez autrement.

Gorgibus. Comment, ces noms étranges ! Ne sont-ce pas vos noms de baptême ?

Magdelon. Mon Dieu, que vous êtes vulgaire ! Pour moi, un de mes étonnements, c'est que vous ayez pu faire
5 une fille si spirituelle que moi. A-t-on jamais parlé dans le beau style de Cathos ni de Magdelon ? et ne m'avouerez-vous pas que ce seroit assez d'un de ces noms pour décrier le plus beau roman du monde ?

Cathos. Il est vrai, mon oncle, qu'une oreille un peu déli-
10 cate pâtit furieusement à entendre prononcer ces mots-là ; et le nom de Polixène que ma cousine a choisi, et celui d'Aminthe que je me suis donné, ont une grâce dont il faut que vous demeuriez d'accord.

Gorgibus. Ecoutez ; il n'y a qu'un mot qui serve. Je
15 n'entends point que vous ayez d'autres noms que ceux qui vous ont été donnés par vos parrains et marraines ; et pour ces messieurs dont il est question, je connois leurs familles et leurs biens, et je veux résolûment que vous vous disposiez à les recevoir pour maris. Je me lasse de vous avoir sur les
20 bras, et la garde de deux filles est une charge un peu trop pesante, pour un homme de mon âge.

Cathos. Pour moi, mon oncle, tout ce que je vous puis dire, c'est que je trouve le mariage une chose tout à fait choquante.

25 *Magdelon.* Souffrez que nous prenions un peu haleine parmi le beau monde de Paris, où nous ne faisons que d'arriver. Laissez-nous faire à loisir le tissu de notre roman, et n'en pressez point tant la conclusion.

Gorgibus. Il n'en faut point douter, elles sont achevées.
30 Encore un coup, je n'entends rien à toutes ces balivernes, je veux être maître absolu, et pour trancher toutes sortes de discours, ou vous serez mariées toutes deux avant qu'il soit peu, ou, ma foi, vous serez religieuses, j'en fais un bon serment.

SCÈNE V.

CATHOS, MAGDELON.

Cathos. Mon Dieu, ma chère, que ton père a la forme enfoncée dans la matière! que son intelligence est épaisse, et qu'il fait sombre dans son âme!

Magdelon. Que veux-tu, ma chère, j'en suis en confusion pour lui. J'ai peine à me persuader que je puisse être vérit- 5 ablement sa fille, et je crois que quelque aventure, un jour, me viendra développer une naissance plus illustre.

Cathos. Je le croirois bien, oui, il y a toutes les apparences du monde, et pour moi, quand je me regarde aussi...

SCÈNE VI.

MAROTTE, CATHOS, MAGDELON.

Marotte. Voilà un laquais qui demande si vous êtes au 10 logis, et dit que son maître vous veut venir voir.

Magdelon. Apprenez, sotte, à vous énoncer moins vulgairement. Dites : voilà un nécessaire qui demande si vous êtes en commodité d'être visibles.

Marotte. Dame, je n'entends point le latin, et je n'ai pas 15 appris, comme vous, la filofie dans *le Grand Cyre.*

Magdelon. L'impertinente ! Le moyen de souffrir cela ! Et qui est-il le maître de ce laquais?

Marotte. Il me l'a nommé le marquis de Mascarille.

Magdelon. Ah, ma chère! un marquis! Oui, allez dire 20 qu'on nous peut voir. C'est sans doute un bel esprit qui aura ouï parler de nous.

Cathos. Assurément, ma chère.

Magdelon. Il faut le recevoir dans cette salle basse, plûtot qu'en notre chambre : ajustons un peu nos cheveux au moins, 25 et soutenons notre réputation. Vite, venez nous tendre ici dedans le conseiller des grâces.

Marotte. Par ma foi, je ne sais point quelle bête c'est là :
il faut parler chrétien, si vouz voulez que je vous entende.

Cathos. Apportez-nous le miroir, ignorante que vous êtes.
Et gardez-vous bien d'en salir la glace par la communication
5 de votre image.

SCÈNE VII.

MASCARILLE, DEUX PORTEURS.

Mascarille. Holà, porteurs, holà ! Là, là, là, là, là, là.
Je pense que ces marauds-là ont dessein de me briser, à
force de heurter contre les murailles et les pavés.

1. *Porteur.* Dame, c'est que la porte est étroite. Vous
10 avez voulu aussi, que nous soyons entrés jusqu'ici.

Mascarille. Je le crois bien. Voudriez-vous, faquins, que
j'exposasse l'embonpoint de mes plumes aux inclémences de
la saison pluvieuse, et que j'allasse imprimer mes souliers en
boue ? Allez, ôtez votre chaise d'ici.

15   2. *Porteur.* Payez-nous donc, s'il vous plaît, Monsieur.

Mascarille. Hem ?

2. *Porteur.* Je dis, monsieur, que vous nous donniez de
l'argent, s'il vous plaît.

Mascarille (lui donnant un soufflet). Comment, coquin,
20 demander de l'argent à une personne de ma qualité ?

2. *Porteur.* Est-ce ainsi qu'on paye les pauvres gens ? et
votre qualité nous donne-t-elle à dîner ?

Mascarille. Ah, ah, ah, je vous apprendrai à vous connoître. Ces canailles-là s'osent jouer à moi.

25   1. *Porteur (prenant un des bâtons de sa chaise).* Çà, payez-
nous vitement !

Mascarille. Quoi ?

1. *Porteur.* Je dis que je veux avoir de l'argent tout à
l'heure.

30   *Mascarille.* Il est raisonnable, celui-là.

1. *Porteur.* Vite donc.

Mascarille. Oui-dà, tu parles comme il faut, toi ; mais l'autre est un coquin qui ne sait ce qu'il dit. Tiens, es-tu content ?

1. *Porteur.* Non, je ne suis pas content, vous avez donné 5 un soufflet à mon camarade, et...

Mascarille. Doucement, tiens, voilà pour le soufflet. On obtient tout de moi quand on s'y prend de la bonne façon. Allez, venez me reprendre tantôt pour aller au Louvre, au petit coucher. 10

SCÈNE VIII.

MAROTTE, MASCARILLE.

Marotte. Monsieur, voilà mes maîtresses qui vont venir tout à l'heure.

Mascarille. Qu'elles ne se pressent point, je suis ici posté commodément pour attendre.

Marotte. Les voici. 15

SCÈNE IX.

MAGDELON, CATHOS, MASCARILLE, ALMANZOR.

Mascarille (*après avoir salué*). Mesdames, vous serez surprises, sans doute, de l'audace de ma visite ; mais votre réputation vous attire cette méchante affaire, et le mérite a, pour moi, des charmes si puissants, que je cours partout après lui. 20

Magdelon. Si vous poursuivez le mérite, ce n'est pas sur nos terres que vous devez chasser.

Cathos. Pour voir chez nous le mérite, il a fallu que vous l'y ayez amené.

Mascarille. Ah ! je m'inscris en faux contre vos paroles. 25 La renommée accuse juste en contant ce que vous valez, et vous allez faire pic, repic et capot, tout ce qu'il y a de galant dans Paris.

Magdelon. Votre complaisance pousse un peu trop avant la libéralité de ses louanges, et nous n'avons garde, ma cou-
5 sine et moi, de donner de notre sérieux dans le doux de votre flatterie.

Cathos. Ma chère, il faudroit faire donner des siéges.

Magdelon. Holà Almanzor.

Almanzor. Madame.

10 *Magdelon.* Vite, voiturez-nous ici les commodités de la conversation.

Mascarille. Mais au moins, y a-t-il sûreté ici pour moi ?

Cathos. Que craignez-vous !

Mascarille. Quelque vol de mon cœur, quelque assassinat
15 de ma franchise. Je vois ici des yeux qui ont la mine d'être de fort mauvais garçons, de faire insulte aux libertés, et de traiter une âme de Turc à More. Comment diable, d'abord qu'on les approche, ils se mettent sur leur garde meurtrière ? Ah ! par ma foi, je m'en défie, et je m'en vais gagner au pied,
20 ou je veux caution bourgeoise qu'ils ne me feront point de mal.

Magdelon. Ma chère, c'est le caractère enjoué.

Cathos. Je vois bien que c'est un Amilcar.

Magdelon. Ne craignez rien, nos yeux n'ont point de
25 mauvais desseins, et votre cœur peut dormir en assurance sur leur prud'homie.

Cathos. Mais de grâce, monsieur, ne soyez pas inexorable à ce fauteuil qui vous tend les bras il y a un quart d'heure ; contentez un peu l'envie qu'il a de vous embrasser.

30 *Mascarille (après s'être peigné et avoir ajusté ses canons).* Eh bien, mesdames, que dites-vous de Paris ?

Magdelon. Hélas ! qu'en pourrions-nous dire ? Il fau-droit être l'antipode de la raison, pour ne pas confesser que Paris est le grand bureau des merveilles, le centre du bon
35 goût, du bel esprit et de la galanterie.

Mascarille. Pour moi, je tiens que hors de Paris, il n'y a point de salut pour les honnêtes gens.

Cathos. C'est une vérité incontestable.

Mascarille. Il y fait un peu crotté, mais nous avons la chaise. 5

Magdelon. Il est vrai que la chaise est un retranchement merveilleux contre les insultes de la boue, et du mauvais temps.

Mascarille. Vous recevez beaucoup de visites? Quel bel-esprit est des vôtres? 10

Magdelon. Hélas! nous ne sommes pas encore connues; mais nous sommes en passe de l'être, et nous avons une amie particulière qui nous a promis d'amener ici tous ces messieurs du Recueil des pièces choisies.

Cathos. Et certains autres qu'on nous a nommés aussi 15 pour être les arbitres souverains des belles choses.

Mascarille. C'est moi qui ferai votre affaire mieux que personne; ils me rendent tous visite, et je puis dire que je ne me lève jamais sans une demi-douzaine de beaux esprits.

Magdelon. Eh! mon Dieu, nous vous serons obligées de 20 la dernière obligation, si vous nous faites cette amitié; car enfin il faut avoir la connoissance de tous ces messieurs-là, si l'on veut être du beau monde. Ce sont eux qui donnent le branle à la réputation dans Paris, et vous savez qu'il y en a tel dont il ne faut que la seule fréquentation pour vous donner 25 bruit de connoisseuse, quand il n'y auroit rien autre chose que cela. Mais pour moi ce que je considère particulièrement, c'est que par le moyen de ces visites spirituelles, on est instruite de cent choses qu'il faut savoir de nécessité, et qui sont de l'essence du bel-esprit. On apprend par là 30 chaque jour les petites nouvelles galantes, les jolis commerces de prose et de vers. On sait à point nommé: un tel a composé la plus jolie pièce du monde sur un tel sujet; une telle a fait des paroles sur un tel air; celui-ci a fait un madrigal sur une jouissance; celui-là a composé des stances 35 sur une infidélité; monsieur un tel écrivit hier au soir un

sixain à mademoiselle une telle, dont elle lui a envoyé la réponse ce matin sur les huit heures ; un tel auteur a fait un tel dessein ; celui-là en est à la troisième partie de son roman ; cet autre met ses ouvrages sous la presse. C'est là ce qui
5 vous fait valoir dans les compagnies ; et si l'on ignore ces choses, je ne donnerois pas un clou de tout l'esprit qu'on peut avoir.

Cathos. En effet, je trouve que c'est renchérir sur le ridicule, qu'une personne se pique d'esprit et ne sache pas jus-
10 qu'au moindre petit quatrain qui se fait chaque jour ; et pour moi j'aurois toutes les hontes du monde s'il falloit qu'on vînt à me demander si j'aurois vu quelque chose de nouveau que je n'aurois pas vu.

Mascarille. Il est vrai qu'il est honteux de n'avoir pas des
15 premiers tout ce qui se fait ; mais ne vous mettez pas en peine, je veux établir chez vous une académie de beaux esprits, et je vous promets qu'il ne se fera pas un bout de vers dans Paris, que vous ne sachiez par cœur avant tous les autres. Pour moi, tel que vous me voyez, je m'en escrime un peu quand je
20 veux ; et vous verrez courir de ma façon, dans les belles ruelles de Paris, deux cents chansons, autant de sonnets, quatre cents épigrammes et plus de mille madrigaux, sans compter les énigmes et les portraits.

Magdelon. Je vous avoue que je suis furieusement pour
25 les portraits ; je ne vois rien de si galant que cela.

Mascarille. Les portraits sont difficiles, et demandent un esprit profond : vous en verrez de ma manière qui ne vous déplairont pas.

Cathos. Pour moi, j'aime terriblement les énigmes.
30 *Mascarille.* Cela exerce l'esprit, et j'en ai fait quatre encore ce matin, que je vous donnerai à deviner.

Magdelon. Les madrigaux sont agréables, quand ils sont bien tournés.

Mascarille. C'est mon talent particulier, et je travaille à
35 mettre en madrigaux toute l'histoire romaine.

Magdelon. Ah! certes, cela sera du dernier beau. J'en retiens un exemplaire au moins, si vous le faites imprimer.

Mascarille. Je vous en promets à chacune un, et des mieux reliés. Cela est au-dessous de ma condition ; mais je le fais seulement pour donner à gagner aux libraires qui me 5 persécutent.

Magdelon. Je m'imagine que le plaisir est grand de se voir imprimé.

Mascarille. Sans doute. Mais à propos, il faut que je vous die un impromptu que je fis hier chez une duchesse de 10 mes amies que je fus visiter ; car je suis diablement fort sur les impromptus.

Cathos. L'impromptu est justement la pierre de touche de l'esprit.

Mascarille. Écoutez donc. 15

Magdelon. Nous y sommes de toutes nos oreilles.

Mascarille :—

> *Oh, oh, je n'y prenois pas garde,*
> *Tandis que, sans songer à mal, je vous regarde,*
> *Votre œil en tapinois me dérobe mon cœur,* 20
> *Au voleur, au voleur, au voleur, au voleur !*

Cathos. Ah, mon Dieu ! voilà qui est poussé dans le dernier galant.

Mascarille. Tout ce que je fais a l'air cavalier, cela ne sent point le pédant. 25

Magdelon. Il en est éloigné de plus de deux mille lieues.

Mascarille. Avez-vous remarqué ce commencement, *oh, oh ?* voilà qui est extraordinaire, *oh, oh.* Comme un homme qui s'avise tout d'un coup, *oh, oh.* La surprise, *oh, oh.*

Magdelon. Oui, je trouve ce *oh, oh,* admirable. 30

Mascarille. Il semble que cela ne soit rien.

Cathos. Ah, mon Dieu, que dites-vous ! Ce sont là de ces sortes de choses qui ne se peuvent payer.

Magdelon. Sans doute ; et j'aimerois mieux avoir fait ce *oh, oh !* qu'un poëme épique. 3⁵

Mascarille. Tu dieu, vous avez le goût bon.

Magdelon. Eh, je ne l'ai pas tout à fait mauvais.

Mascarille. Mais n'admirez-vous pas aussi *je n'y prenois pas garde ? je n'y prenois pas garde*, je ne m'apercevois pas de cela, façon de parler naturelle, *je n'y prenois pas garde. Tandis que sans songer à mal.* Tandis qu'innocemment, sans malice, comme un pauvre mouton, *je vous regarde* ; c'est-à-dire, je m'amuse à vous considérer, je vous observe, je vous contemple. *Votre œil en tapinois...* Que vous semble de ce mot *tapinois*, n'est-il pas bien choisi ?

Cathos. Tout à fait bien.

Mascarille. Tapinois, en cachette : il semble que ce soit un chat qui vienne de prendre une souris. *Tapinois.*

Magdelon. Il ne se peut rien de mieux.

Mascarille. Me dérobe mon cœur, me l'emporte, me le ravit. *Au voleur, au voleur, au voleur, au voleur !* Ne diriez-vous pas que c'est un homme qui crie et court après un voleur pour le faire arrêter, *Au voleur, au voleur, au voleur, au voleur !*

Magdelon. Il faut avouer que cela a un tour spirituel et galant.

Mascarille. Je veux vous dire l'air que j'ai fait dessus.

Cathos. Vous avez appris la musique ?

Mascarille. Moi ? Point du tout.

Cathos. Et comment donc cela se peut-il ?

Mascarille. Les gens de qualité savent tout sans avoir jamais rien appris.

Magdelon. Assurément, ma chère.

Mascarille. Écoutez si vous trouverez l'air à votre goût : *hem, hem, la, la, la, la, la.* La brutalité de la saison a furieusement outragé la délicatesse de ma voix ; mais il n'importe, c'est à la cavalière.

(Il chante :)

    Oh, oh, je n'y prenois pas...

Cathos. Ah, que voilà un air qui est passionné! Est-ce qu'on n'en meurt point?

Magdelon. Il y a de la chromatique là dedans.

Mascarille. Ne trouvez-vous pas la pensée bien exprimée dans le chant? *Au voleur!...* Et puis, comme si l'on crioit bien fort, *au, au, au, au, au, au voleur!* Et tout d'un coup, comme une personne essoufflée, *au voleur.*

Magdelon. C'est là savoir le fin des choses, le grand fin, le fin du fin. Tout est merveilleux, je vous assure; je suis enthousiasmée de l'air et des paroles.

Cathos. Je n'ai encore rien vu de cette force-là.

Mascarille. Tout ce que je fais me vient naturellement, c'est sans étude.

Magdelon. La nature vous a traité en vraie mère passionnée, et vous en êtes l'enfant gâté.

Mascarille. A quoi donc passez-vous le temps?

Cathos. A rien du tout.

Magdelon. Nous avons été jusqu'ici dans un jeûne effroyable de divertissements.

Mascarille. Je m'offre à vous mener l'un de ces jours à la comédie, si vous voulez, aussi bien on en doit jouer une nouvelle que je serai bien aise que nous voyions ensemble.

Magdelon. Cela n'est pas de refus.

Mascarille. Mais je vous demande d'applaudir comme il faut, quand nous serons là. Car je me suis engagé de faire valoir la pièce, et l'auteur m'en est venu prier encore ce matin. C'est la coutume ici qu'à nous autres gens de condition, les auteurs viennent lire leurs pièces nouvelles, pour nous engager à les trouver belles, et leur donner de la réputation, et je vous laisse à penser si, quand nous disons quelque chose, le parterre ose nous contredire. Pour moi, j'y suis fort exact; et quand j'ai promis à quelque poëte, je crie toujours, voilà qui est beau, devant que les chandelles soient allumées.

Magdelon. Ne m'en parlez point, c'est un admirable lieu

F

que Paris ; il s'y passe cent choses tous les jours qu'on ignore dans les provinces, quelque spirituelle qu'on puisse être.

Cathos. C'est assez, puisque nous sommes instruites, nous ferons notre devoir de nous écrier comme il faut sur tout ce
5 qu'on dira.

Mascarille. Je ne sais si je me trompe ; mais vous avez toute la mine d'avoir fait quelque comédie.

Magdelon. Eh, il pourroit être quelque chose de ce que vous dites.

10 *Mascarille.* Ah, ma foi, il faudra que nous la voyions. Entre nous, j'en ai composé une que je veux faire représenter.

Cathos. Hé, à quels comédiens la donnerez-vous ?

Mascarille. Belle demande ! Aux grands comédiens ; il
15 n'y a qu'eux qui soient capables de faire valoir les choses ; les autres sont des ignorants qui récitent comme l'on parle, ils ne savent pas faire ronfler les vers et s'arrêter au bel endroit ; et le moyen de connoître où est le beau vers, si le comédien ne s'y arrête, et ne vous avertit par là qu'il faut
20 faire le brouhaha ?

Cathos. En effet, il y a manière de faire sentir aux auditeurs les beautés d'un ouvrage, et les choses ne valent que ce qu'on les fait valoir.

Mascarille. Que vous semble de ma petite-oie? La
25 trouvez-vous congruante à l'habit ?

Cathos. Tout à fait.

Mascarille. Le ruban est bien choisi.

Magdelon. Furieusement bien. C'est Perdrigeon tout pur.

30 *Mascarille.* Que dites-vous de mes canons ?

Magdelon. Ils ont tout à fait bon air.

Mascarille. Je puis me vanter au moins qu'ils ont un grand quartier plus que tous ceux qu'on fait.

Magdelon. Il faut avouer que je n'ai jamais vu porter si
35 haut l'élégance de l'ajustement.

Mascarille. Attachez un peu sur ces gants la réflexion de votre odorat.

Magdelon. Ils sentent terriblement bon.

Cathos. Je n'ai jamais respiré une odeur mieux conditionnée. 5

Mascarille. Et celle-là ?

(*Il donne à sentir les cheveux poudrés de sa perruque.*)

Magdelon. Elle est tout à fait de qualité ; le sublime en est touché délicieusement.

Mascarille. Vous ne me dites rien de mes plumes, comment les trouvez-vous ? 10

Cathos. Effroyablement belles.

Mascarille. Savez-vous que le brin me coûte un louis d'or ? Pour moi, j'ai cette manie de vouloir donner généralement sur tout ce qu'il y a de plus beau. 15

Magdelon. Je vous assure que nous sympathisons vous et moi, j'ai une délicatesse furieuse pour tout ce que je porte ; et jusqu'à mes chaussettes, je ne puis rien souffrir qui ne soit de la bonne ouvrière.

Mascarille (s'écriant brusquement). Ahi, ahi, ahi, douce- 20 ment ; Dieu me damne, mesdames, c'est fort mal en user ; j'ai à me plaindre de votre procédé ; cela n'est pas honnête.

Cathos. Qu'est-ce donc ? qu'avez-vous ?

Mascarille. Quoi, toutes deux contre mon cœur, en même temps ? m'attaquer à droite et à gauche ? Ah ! c'est contre le 25 droit des gens, la partie n'est pas égale, et je m'en vais crier au meurtre.

Cathos. Il faut avouer qu'il dit les choses d'une manière particulière.

Magdelon. Il a un tour admirable dans l'esprit. 30

Cathos. Vous avez plus de peur que de mal, et votre cœur crie avant qu'on l'écorche.

Mascarille. Comment diable ! il est écorché depuis la tête jusqu'aux pieds.

SCÈNE X.

MAROTTE, MASCARILLE, CATHOS, MAGDELON.

Marotte. Madame, on demande à vous voir.

Magdelon. Qui?

Marotte. Le vicomte de Jodelet.

Mascarille. Le vicomte de Jodelet?

5 *Marotte.* Oui, Monsieur.

Cathos. Le connoissez-vous?

Mascarille. C'est mon meilleur ami.

Magdelon. Faites entrer vitement.

Mascarille. Il y a quelque temps que nous ne nous
10 sommes vus, et je suis ravi de cette aventure.

Cathos. Le voici.

SCÈNE XI.

JODELET, MASCARILLE, CATHOS, MAGDELON,
MAROTTE, ALMANZOR.

Mascarille. Ah, vicomte!

Jodelet (*s'embrassant l'un et l'autre*). Ah, marquis!

Mascarille. Que je suis aise de te rencontrer!

15 *Jodelet.* Que j'ai de joie de te voir ici!

Mascarille. Baise-moi donc encore un peu, je te prie.

Magdelon. Ma toute bonne, nous commençons d'être
connues, voilà le beau monde qui prend le chemin de nous
venir voir.

20 *Mascarille.* Mesdames, agréez que je vous présente ce
gentilhomme-ci. Sur ma parole, il est digne d'être connu
de vous.

Jodelet. Il est juste de venir vous rendre ce qu'on vous
doit, et vos attraits exigent leurs droits seigneuriaux sur
25 toutes sortes de personnes.

Magdelon. C'est pousser vos civilités jusqu'aux derniers confins de la flatterie.

Cathos. Cette journée doit être marquée dans notre almanach, comme une journée bienheureuse.

Magdelon. Allons, petit garçon, faut-il toujours vous ré- 5 péter les choses? Voyez-vous pas qu'il faut le surcroît d'un fauteuil?

Mascarille. Ne vous étonnez pas de voir le Vicomte de la sorte, il ne fait que sortir d'une maladie, qui lui a rendu le visage pâle comme vous le voyez. 10

Jodelet. Ce sont fruits des veilles de la cour, et des fatigues de la guerre.

Mascarille. Savez-vous, mesdames, que vous voyez dans le Vicomte un des vaillants hommes du siècle? C'est un brave à trois poils. 15

Jodelet. Vous ne m'en devez rien, Marquis, et nous savons ce que vous savez faire aussi.

Mascarille. Il est vrai que nous nous sommes vus tous deux dans l'occasion.

Jodelet. Et dans des lieux où il faisoit fort chaud. 20

Mascarille (les regardant toutes deux). Oui, mais non pas si chaud qu'ici. Hai, hai, hai.

Jodelet. Notre connoissance s'est faite à l'armée, et la première fois que nous nous vîmes, il commandoit un régiment de cavalerie sur les galères de Malte. 25

Mascarille. Il est vrai; mais vous étiez pourtant dans l'emploi avant que j'y fusse, et je me souviens que je n'étois que petit officier encore, que vous commandiez deux mille chevaux.

Jodelet. La guerre est une belle chose; mais, ma foi, la 30 cour récompense bien mal aujourd'hui les gens de service comme nous.

Mascarille. C'est ce qui fait que je veux pendre l'épée au croc.

Cathos.   Pour moi, j'ai un furieux tendre pour les hommes d'épée.

Magdelon.   Je les aime aussi, mais je veux que l'esprit assaisonne la bravoure.

5   *Mascarille.*   Te souvient-il, Vicomte, de cette demi-lune que nous emportâmes sur les ennemis au siége d'Arras?

Jodelet.   Que veux-tu dire avec ta demi-lune? C'étoit bien une lune toute entière.

Mascarille.   Je pense que tu as raison.

10   *Jodelet.*   Il m'en doit bien souvenir, ma foi; j'y fus blessé à la jambe d'un coup de grenade, dont je porte encore les marques. Tâtez un peu, de grâce; vous sentirez quel coup c'étoit là.

Cathos.   Il est vrai que la cicatrice est grande.

15   *Mascarille.*   Donnez-moi un peu votre main, et tâtez celui-ci, là, justement au derrière de la tête. Y êtes-vous?

Magdelon.   Oui, je sens quelque chose.

Mascarille.   C'est un coup de mousquet que je reçus la dernière campagne que j'ai faite.

20   *Jodelet.*   Voici un autre coup qui me perça de part en part à l'attaque de Gravelines.

Mascarille.   Ce sont des marques honorables, qui font voir ce qu'on est.

Cathos.   Nous ne doutons point de ce que vous êtes.

25   *Mascarille.*   Vicomte, as-tu là ton carrosse?

Jodelet.   Pourquoi?

Mascarille.   Nous mènerions promener ces dames hors des portes, et leur donnerions un cadeau.

Magdelon.   Nous ne saurions sortir aujourd'hui.

30   *Mascarille.*   Ayons donc les violons pour danser.

Jodelet.   Ma foi, c'est bien avisé.

Magdelon.   Pour cela, nous y consentons; mais il faut donc quelque surcroît de compagnie.

Mascarille. Holà! Champagne, Picard, Bourguignon, Cascaret, Basque, la Verdure, Lorrain, Provençal, la Violette. Au diable soient tous les laquais. Je ne pense pas qu'il y ait gentilhomme en France plus mal servi que moi. Ces canailles me laissent toujours seul. 5

Magdelon. Almanzor, dites aux gens de monsieur qu'ils aillent querir des violons, et nous faites venir ces messieurs et ces dames d'ici près, pour peupler la solitude de notre bal.

Mascarille. Vicomte, que dis-tu de ces yeux?

Jodelet. Mais toi-même, marquis, que t'en semble? 10

Mascarille. Moi, je dis que nos libertés auront peine à sortir d'ici les braies nettes. Au moins, pour moi, je reçois d'étranges secousses, et mon cœur ne tient plus qu'à un filet.

Magdelon. Que tout ce qu'il dit est naturel! Il tourne les choses le plus agréablement du monde. 15

Cathos. Il est vrai qu'il fait une furieuse dépense en esprit.

Mascarille. Pour vous montrer que je suis véritable, je veux faire un impromptu là-dessus.

Cathos. Eh, je vous en conjure de toute la dévotion de 20 mon cœur. Que nous ayons quelque chose qu'on ait fait pour nous.

Jodelet. J'aurois envie d'en faire autant: mais je me trouve un peu incommodé de la veine poétique, pour la quantité des saignées que j'y ai faites ces jours passés. 25

Mascarille. Que diable est cela? je fais toujours bien le premier vers; mais j'ai peine à faire les autres. Ma foi, ceci est un peu trop pressé; je vous ferai un impromptu à loisir, que vous trouverez le plus beau du monde.

Jodelet. Il a de l'esprit comme un démon. 30

Magdelon. Et du galant, et du bien tourné.

Mascarille. Vicomte, dis-moi un peu, y a-t-il longtemps que tu n'as vu la comtesse?

Jodelet. Il y a plus de trois semaines que je ne lui ai rendu visite. 35

Mascarille. Sais-tu bien que le duc m'est venu voir ce matin, et m'a voulu mener à la campagne courir un cerf avec lui?

Magdelon. Voici nos amies qui viennent.

SCÈNE XII.

JODELET, MASCARILLE, CATHOS, MAGDELON, MAROTTE, LUCILE.

5 *Magdelon.* Mon Dieu, mes chères, nous vous demandons pardon. Ces messieurs ont eu fantaisie de nous donner les âmes des pieds; et nous vous avons envoyé querir pour remplir les vuides de notre assemblé.

Lucile. Vous nous avez obligées sans doute.

10 *Mascarille.* Ce n'est ici qu'un bal à la hâte; mais l'un de ces jours nous vous en donnerons un dans les formes. Les violons sont-ils venus?

Almanzor. Oui, monsieur, ils sont ici.

Cathos. Allons donc, mes chères, prenez place.

15 *Mascarille (dansant lui seul comme par prélude).* La, la, la, la, la, la, la, la.

Magdelon. Il a tout à fait la taille élégante.

Cathos. Et a la mine de danser proprement.

Mascarille (ayant pris Magdelon). Ma franchise va
20 danser la courante aussi bien que mes pieds. En cadence, violons, en cadence. O quels ignorants! Il n'y a pas moyen de danser avec eux; le diable vous emporte, ne sauriez-vous jouer en mesure? La, la, la, la, la, la, la, la. Ferme, ô violons de village.

25 *Jodelet (dansant ensuite).* Holà! ne pressez pas si fort la cadence, je ne fais que sortir de maladie.

SCÈNE XIII.

'Du Croisy, La Grange, et les précédents.

La Grange (*un bâton à la main*). Ah, ah, coquins, que faites-vous ici? il y a trois heures que nous vous cherchons.

Mascarille (*se sentant battre*). Ahy, ahy, ahy, vous ne m'aviez pas dit que les coups en seroient aussi.

Jodelet. Ahy, ahy, ahy.   5

La Grange. C'est bien à vous, infâme que vous êtes, à vouloir faire l'homme d'importance.

Du Croisy. Voilà qui vous apprendra à vous connoître.

(*Ils sortent.*)

SCÈNE XIV.

MASCARILLE, JODELET, CATHOS, MAGDELON.

Magdelon. Que veut donc dire ceci?   10

Jodelet. C'est une gageure.

Cathos. Quoi, vous laisser battre de la sorte?

Mascarille. Mon Dieu, je n'ai pas voulu faire semblant de rien : car je suis violent, et je me serois emporté.

Magdelon. Endurer un affront comme celui-là, en notre 15 présence !

Mascarille. Ce n'est rien, ne laissons pas d'achever. Nous nous connoissons il y a longtemps ; et entre amis, on ne va pas se piquer pour si peu de chose.

SCÈNE XV.

Du Croisy, La Grange, Mascarille, Jodelet,
Magdelon, Cathos.

La Grange. Ma foi, marauds, vous ne vous rirez pas de nous, je vous promets. Entrez, vous autres.

(Trois ou quatre spadassins entrent.)

Magdelon. Quelle est donc cette audace, de venir nous
5 troubler de la sorte dans notre maison?

Du Croisy. Comment, mesdames, nous endurerons que nos laquais soient mieux reçus que nous? qu'ils viennent vous faire l'amour à nos dépens, et vous donnent le bal?

Magdelon. Vos laquais?

10 *La Grange.* Oui, nos laquais, et cela n'est ni beau ni honnête de nous les débaucher comme vous faites.

Magdelon. O Ciel, quelle insolence!

La Grange. Mais ils n'auront pas l'avantage de se servir de nos habits pour vous donner dans la vue, et si vous les
15 voulez aimer, ce sera, ma foi, pour leurs beaux yeux. Vite, qu'on les dépouille sur-le-champ.

Jodelet. Adieu notre braverie.

Mascarille. Voilà le marquisat et la vicomté à bas.

Du Croisy. Ha, ha, coquins, vous avez l'audace d'aller sur
20 nos brisées. Vous irez chercher autre part de quoi vous rendre agréables aux yeux de vos belles, je vous en assure.

La Grange. C'est trop que de nous supplanter, et de nous supplanter avec nos propres habits.

Mascarille. O Fortune, quelle est ton inconstance!

25 *Du Croisy.* Vite, qu'on leur ôte jusqu'à la moindre chose.

La Grange. Qu'on emporte toutes ces hardes, dépêchez. Maintenant, mesdames, en l'état qu'ils sont, vous pouvez continuer vos amours avec eux tant qu'il vous plaira, nous vous laissons toute sorte de liberté pour cela, et nous vous

protestons, monsieur et moi, que nous n'en serons aucune-
ment jaloux.

Cathos. Ah, quelle confusion !

Magdelon. Je crève de dépit.

Un des Violons, au Marquis. Qu'est-ce donc que ceci ? 5
Qui nous payera, nous autres ?

Mascarille. Demandez à Monsieur le Vicomte.

Un des Violons, au Vicomte. Qui est-ce qui nous donnera
de l'argent ?

Jodelet. Demandez à Monsieur le Marquis. 10

SCÈNE XVI.

GORGIBUS, MASCARILLE, MAGDELON.

Gorgibus. Ah, coquines que vous êtes, vous nous mettez
dans beaux draps blancs, à ce que je vois, et je viens d'apprendre de belles affaires, vraiment, de ces messieurs qui
sortent.

Magdelon. Ah, mon père, c'est une pièce sanglante qu'ils 15
nous ont faite.

Gorgibus. Oui, c'est une pièce sanglante ; mais qui est
un effet de votre impertinence, infâmes. Ils se sont ressentis
du traitement que vous leur avez fait, et cependant, mal-
heureux que je suis, il faut que je boive l'affront. 20

Magdelon. Ah, je jure que nous en serons vengées, ou que
je mourrai en la peine. Et vous, marauds, osez-vous vous
tenir ici après votre insolence ?

Mascarille. Traiter comme cela un marquis ? Voilà ce
que c'est que du monde, la moindre disgrâce nous fait mé- 25
priser de ceux qui nous chérissoient. Allons, camarade,
allons chercher fortune autre part ; je vois bien qu'on n'aime
ici que la vaine apparence, et qu'on n'y considère point la
vertu toute nue. (*Ils sortent tous deux.*)

SCÈNE XVII.

GORGIBUS, MAGDELON, CATHOS, Violons.

Violons. Monsieur, nous entendons que vous nous con-
tentiez à leur défaut pour ce que nous avons joué ici.

Gorgibus, les battant. Oui, oui, je vous vais contenter, et
voici la monnoie dont je vous veux payer. Et vous, pen-
5 dardes, je ne sais qui me tient que je ne vous en fasse autant.
Nous allons servir de fable, et de risée à tout le monde, et
voilà ce que vous vous êtes attiré par vos extravagances.
Allez vous cacher, vilaines ; allez vous cacher pour jamais.
Et vous, qui êtes cause de leur folie, sottes billevesées, per-
10 nicieux amusements des esprits oisifs, romans, vers, chansons, sonnets et sonnettes, puissiez-vous être à tous les
diables !

NOTES.

P. 48, l. 3. Dramatis Personæ. *Gorgibus.* Apparently the name is older than Molière's use of it for a ludicrous personage.

l. 5. *Cathos.* Short for Catherine, pronounced *Catau.*

l. 7. *Almanzor.* These *Précieuses* have named their lacquey after one of the characters in Gomberville's romance of *Polexandre.*

P. 49, l. 18. Preface. *à la chandelle*, alluding to the proverb, 'Cette femme est belle à la chandelle,' beautiful by candle-light. Molière means that plays which act well may not stand being read in the study.

l. 20. *Galerie du Palais.* Here were the shops of most of the publishers.

l. 24. *On m'a fait voir*, etc. Molière's right in his play was threatened by the piratical publisher, Ribou.

P. 51, l. 11. Scene i. *pecque*, 'silly girl.'

P. 52, l. 6. *ambigu*, 'dubious mixture.'

P. 53, l. 9. Scene iii. *lait virginal*, a cosmetic of the period, the recipe for which is superfluous. Our English ancestresses of the period used the fat of a young dog. (*A Queen's Delight*, 1666.)

brimborions (derived by Littré from *breviarium*), 'a trifle,' 'a thing of no importance.'

l. 11. *lard.* Scarron also, in 1649, laughed at the ladies of his time for their abuse of pommades, *lard et pieds de mouton*, home-made cosmetics.

l. 25. **Scene iv.** *débuter d'abord par le mariage*; modern manners have come round to the ideas of Magdelon on this important subject.

P. 54, l. 16. *Cyrus, Clélie.* Mlle. de Scudéry's long novels are alluded to; each consists of at least ten volumes. Mlle. de Rambouillet's love affair with M. de Montausier lasted till the lady was thirty-eight; the courtship had gone on for thirteen years, a 'long wooing.'

l. 22. *pousser.* The word, used in this sense, was one of the fashionable affectations of the day.

l. 24. *temple.* The word *église* was carefully avoided on the stage.

P. 55, l. 5. *les enlèvements.* In the *Grand Cyrus* Mandane is carried off several times. On the *enlèvement* of Mlle. de Boutteville by M. de Coligny, Sarrasin wrote a *ballade*, with the refrain *Qu'il n'est rien tel que d'enlever.*

l. 11. *rien de plus marchand*, more contemporary jargon, in contempt of trade.

l. 16. *donne dans le vrai de la chose.* A phrase much to the taste of the *Précieuses*; it means 'is utterly right.'

l. 19. *la carte de Tendre,* an imaginary map of 'Love's land,' in the *Clélie. Billets-doux, jolis-vers,* and so on, are stages on the road which leads to *Tendre-sur-Estime.* The Abbé d'Aubignac, and Mlle. de Scudéry, disputed the honour of having invented this amorous geography.

l. 24. *une jambe tout unie,* etc. To understand the kind of dress which Cathos liked in an adorer, it is almost necessary to examine the contemporary illustrations of Molière's plays. Here the Marquis de Mascarille wears a long curled periwig, a long embroidered coat reaching nearly to the knees, sleeves slashed and prodigiously puffed at the shoulder, with two tiers of ruffles, and ribbons, slashed and puffed breeches of immense width, wide bell-mouthed frills beneath the knees, and gigantic ribbons in the shoes. A very small sword, and a hat covered with plumes, complete his costume. Illustrations of *L'École des Maris* show Valère in the same costume, much less exaggerated. The dress of Mascarille is also described by Mlle. de Jardins in *Le Récit de la Farce des Précieuses.* See Introduction.

l. 29. *rabats,* collars which were spread out to an absurd breadth.

l. 30. *hauts-de-chausses,* breeches from the belt to the knee, then worn very wide.

l. 33. *baragouin,* 'jargon.'

l. 36. *nous appelez autrement.* The *Précieuses* had commonly an adopted name, usually an anagram of the real name; as *Arthénice* for *Catherine,* in the case of Mme. de Rambouillet.

P. 56, l. 11. *Polixène,* from a novel by Molière (not Poquelin).

Aminthe, from a novel, *Polexandre,* by Gomberville.

l. 30. *balivernes* = childish nonsense.

P. 57, l. 1. Scene v. *ma chère,* this familiar address was then an affectation.

la forme enfoncée, a tag of scholastic philosophy.

l. 6. *que quelque aventure.* Magdelon hopes she will prove to have been changed at nurse, and to be really of a noble lineage, like the heroines in her favourite novels.

l. 13. Scene vi. *un nécessaire,* used by the *Précieuses* to mean a servant.

l. 27. *le conseiller des grâces.* This term for a mirror is far-fetched indeed, being apparently as old as Martial's *consilium formae speculum* (ix. 17).

P. 58, l. 2. *parler chrétien,* this use of 'Christian' to mean 'like an ordinary person,' is as common in England as in France.

l. 14. Scene vii. Chairs carried by porters had not long been in common use.   Furetière, in the *Roman Bourgeois,* gives a melancholy account of the filth of the streets of Paris, two or three years after the production of the *Précieuses.*   A chair or a carriage was necessary to every one who wished to pay a visit without being splashed from head to foot.   See Scene ix.

l. 25. *Ça, payez-nous vitement.*   Lekain is said to have once acted this little part with extraordinary vigour, so as to strike terror in those who heard him.

l. 30. *Il est raisonnable celui-là!* seems the more comic and characteristic reading.

P. 59, l. 10. *petit coucher,* the interval between the time when the King said good night, and the moment when he actually went to bed.

P. 60, l. 1. **Scene ix.** *pic, repic, capot,* various terms of the game of *Piquet: capot* gains forty points.

l. 10. *voiturez ici,* etc., more jargon for 'bring chairs.'

l. 17. *de Turc à More,* 'as the Turks, in Africa, treat their Moorish subjects.'

l. 19. *gagner au pied,* 'take to my heels.'

l. 20. *caution bourgeoise,* a legal term for sound security.

l. 23. *Amilcar,* a lively Carthaginian gentleman, in the romance of *Clélie.*

l. 30. *après s'être peigné,* the mode of the day authorised all this.

canons were a kind of funnel-shaped articles, widening out from the knee, and ornamented with lace.

P. 61, l. 14. *Recueil des pièces choisies.*   There were two collections of those fugitive pieces, one in prose, one in verse.   Cotin, the Trissotin of Molière's *Femmes Savantes,* wrote much in the collection of verse.

l. 36. *sur une infidélité.*   Verses on all those topics appeared in the *Poésies Choisies.*

P. 62, l. 1. *un sixain.*   A brief snatch of verse in a certain form.

l. 21. *ruelles.*   Originally the space between the bed and the wall, where ladies received their morning visitors.   The bedroom retained the name of *ruelle* after this singular custom became obsolete.

l. 23. *énigmes.*   The Abbé Cotin was very fertile in these compositions.

portraits.   Short sketches of real people, written in prose.   The fashion for these things was at its height in 1659.

l. 35. *l'histoire Romaine en madrigaux.*   Benserade afterwards 'did' the Metamorphoses of Ovid into Rondeaux, but Mascarille attempted a higher flight.

P. 65, l. 1. *Est-ce qu'on n'en meurt point?* an affected expression then in fashion.

l. 3. *de la chromatique,* an example of 'the higher criticism' in music, with no particular meaning.

l. 33. *chandelles.* There were no foot-lights, only candles in lustres hung from the roof. Occasionally the lustre had to be let down, and the candles snuffed.

P. 66, l. 14. *Aux grands comédiens.* The Troupe Royale of the Hôtel de Bourgogne. See Biography of Molière. This is the first indication of his dislike of their pompous declamation. See also *L'Impromptu de Versailles,* and the *Critique de l'École des Femmes.*

l. 24. *petite-oie*: all the frippery of contemporary dress was so called.

l. 28. *Perdrigeon tout pur.* Perdrigeon, according to Bret, was a fashionable tradesman of the period.

l. 33. *quartier,* the fourth of an ell. Mascarille's huge *canons* may be studied in contemporary engravings of this scene, as in editions of 1682. The pictures of Punt, Boucher, Moreau, and others represent the dress of a later period.

P. 67, l. 18. *chaussette,* a sort of footless stocking.

P. 69, l. 10. Scene xi. *le visage pâle.* Jodelet the actor (his real name was Bedeau) seems to have been really ill, and probably pale, at this time.

l. 15. *à trois poils,* the origin of this expression is disputed.

P. 70, l. 6. *siége d'Arras,* in 1654, or the earlier siege of 1640. The latter date would make the two warriors rather elderly men.

l. 21. *Gravelines*; taken from the Spaniards in 1658. There was an earlier siege, 1644.

l. 28. *cadeau,* a collation, an entertainment.

P. 71, l. 1. *Holà, Champagne,* etc.: this is copied from *Le Parasite,* by Tristan L'Hermite, 1654.

l. 12. *les braies nettes,* 'safe and sound.'

P. 72, l. 7. Scene xii. *les âmes des pieds,* 'fiddles.'

P. 73, l. 1. Scene xiii. La Grange, in the stage direction of 1682, has a *bâton* in his hand. This favourite stage weapon, from which Molière received in his time so many blows, appears to have been lined with baize to deaden the strokes.

P. 74, l. 17. Scene xv. *braverie,* 'magnificence.'

l. 25. *qu'on leur ôte,* etc. The 'business' was to strip Jodelet of a number of vests, assumed to hide his leanness. At last he appeared in the guise of a cook.

THE END.

LaVergne, TN USA
12 December 2010
208411LV00003B/9/P